IMAGES OF WAR

HELL IN THE CENTRAL PACIFIC 1944

THE PALAU ISLANDS

RARE PHOTOGRAPHS FROM WARTIME ARCHIVES

Jon Diamond

Pen & Sword
MILITARY

First published in Great Britain in 2020 by
PEN & SWORD MILITARY
An imprint of
Pen & Sword Books Ltd
47 Church Street
Barnsley
South Yorkshire
S70 2AS

ISBN 978-1-52676-216-0

A CIP catalogue record for this book is available from the British Library.

Typeset by Concept, Huddersfield, West Yorkshire, HD4 5JL.
Printed and bound in the UK by CPI Group (UK) Ltd, Croydon, CR0 4YY.

FSC www.fsc.org MIX Paper from responsible sources FSC® C013604

Pen & Sword Books Limited incorporates the imprints of Atlas, Archaeology, Aviation, Discovery, Family History, Fiction, History, Maritime, Military, Military Classics, Politics, Select, Transport, True Crime, Air World, Frontline Publishing, Leo Cooper, Remember When, Seaforth Publishing, The Praetorian Press, Wharncliffe Local History, Wharncliffe Transport, Wharncliffe True Crime and White Owl.

For a complete list of Pen & Sword titles please contact
PEN & SWORD BOOKS LIMITED
47 Church Street, Barnsley, South Yorkshire S70 2AS, England
E-mail: enquiries@pen-and-sword.co.uk
Website: www.pen-and-sword.co.uk

Contents

Acknowledgements

This archival photograph volume in the 'Images of War' series is dedicated to the Armed Forces service members who fought, were wounded and perished during the Palau Islands campaign on Peleliu and Angaur. We ponder upon viewing these photographs about the heroic sacrifice made to maintain freedom, lest we forget under horrific climatic and terrain conditions against a determined suicidal foe.

The author is indebted to the able assistance of the archivists at both the Still Photo Section of the National Archives and Records Administration (NARA) in College Park, Maryland and the United States Army Military History Institute (USAMHI) at the United States Army War College in Carlisle, Pennsylvania. Their diligence is much appreciated as they maintain and safeguard these historic images.

Abbreviations

AA – Anti-aircraft
AAA – Anti-aircraft artillery
AIF – Australian Imperial Force
AP – Armour-piercing
AT – Anti-tank
BAR – Browning Automatic Rifle
C-in-C – Commander-in-Chief
CINCPOA – Commander-in-Chief, Pacific Ocean Areas
CNO – Chief of Naval Operations
COS – Chief of Staff
CP – Command Post
CPA – Central Pacific Area
CSA – Confederate States of America
DP – Dual Purpose
ETO – European Theatre of Operations
GMC – Gun Motor Carriage
HE – High-Explosive
HMC – Howitzer Motor Carriage
HMG – Heavy Machine Gun
HQ – Headquarters
IJA – Imperial Japanese Army
IJN – Imperial Japanese Navy
IMB – Independent Mixed Brigade
LCI – Landing Craft Infantry
LCM – Landing Craft, Mechanized
LCVP – Landing Craft, Vehicle Personnel
LMG – Light machine gun
LOC – Lines of Communication
LSM – Landing Ship Medium
LST – Landing Ship Tank
LVT – Landing Vehicle Tracked
LVT(A) – Landing Vehicle Tracked (Armoured)
M&P – Military & Police
MAG – Marine Air Groups
MAW – Marine Aircraft Wing
MMG – Medium machine gun
NEI – Netherlands East Indies
OP – Observation Post
PFC – Private First Class
PoW – Prisoner of War
RAN – Royal Australian Navy
RCT – Regimental Combat Team
SB – Stretcher-bearer
SBD – Scout Bomber Douglas
SCR – Signal Corps Radio
SMG – Sub-machine gun
SNLF – Special Naval Landing Force
SPA – South Pacific Area
SWPA – Southwest Pacific Area
TB – Tank Battalion
TD – Tank Destroyer
TF – Task Force
TNT – Tri Nitro Toluene
USAAF – United States Army Air Force
USAFFE – United States Army Forces in the Far East
USMC – United States Marine Corps
USN – United States Navy
USNR – United States Naval Reserve
IMAC – I Marine Amphibious Corps
IIIAC III – Amphibious Corps
VAC – V Amphibious Corps

Chapter One

Strategic Prelude to the Palau Islands Campaign

Imperial Japan's Pacific Expansion as a First World War Allied Nation

In 1899, Kaiser Wilhelm's naval forces secured most of the islands in the Caroline, Marshall and Mariana groups by purchasing them from Spain. When the First World War began, Japan, while supporting the Allies, seized all the German holdings in Asia and the Pacific, while other former German islands north of the equator, such as Saipan in the Marianas, were mandated to Imperial Japan at the Treaty of Versailles in 1919. In addition to being on a land war footing in China since 1931, this massive Pacific Ocean territorial acquisition during and after the First World War provided the Imperial Japanese Army (IJA) and Imperial Japanese Navy (IJN) with strategically-located oceanic bases. Specifically, Truk in the Eastern and the Palau Islands in Western Carolines; Kwajalein, Majuro and Jaluit Atolls in the Marshall Islands; and Saipan in the Marianas had been secretly fortified with garrisons and airfields during the interwar years to potentially control Pacific sea lanes as well as ultimately launch the December 1941 attacks against Pearl Harbor, Wake Island, the Philippines, Guam, the Gilbert Islands (Tarawa and Makin Atolls), and Rabaul on New Britain Island in the Australian-mandated territory of New Guinea.

Japanese 'Blitzkrieg' Across the Pacific Ocean

The IJA and IJN were victorious across the Asian continent, the Philippine and Netherland East Indies (NEI) Archipelagos, Malaya and Singapore, Hong Kong, New Britain, the northern coasts of Northeast New Guinea and Papua as well as many island groups across the Central and South Pacific from December 1941 through to June 1942 (see Map 1). The 'high-water mark' of the Japanese conquests was preceded by three unrelated engagements with the US Navy (USN). First, on 18 April 1942, Vice Admiral William F. 'Bull' Halsey's Task Force (TF)-16 launched sixteen B-25B Mitchell medium bombers of the United States Army Air Force's (USAAF)

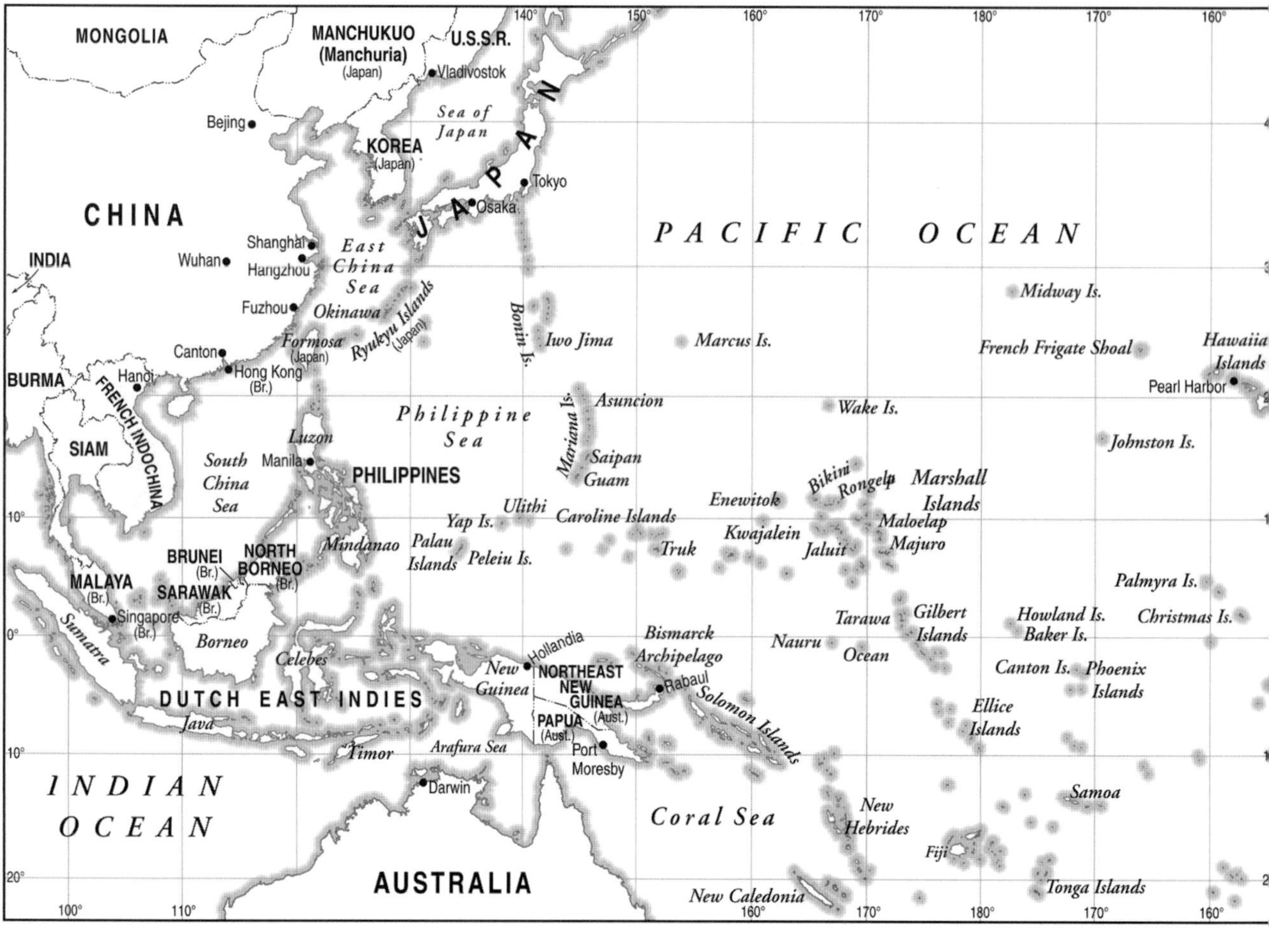

Map 1. Strategic Overview of the Pacific War, 1941–1942. After the IJN attack on Pearl Harbor, Malaya and the Philippine Islands were invaded in December 1941. Malaya was soon conquered by the IJA 25th Army with Singapore falling on 15 February 1942. Filipino-American forces surrendered on Luzon's Bataan Peninsula in April 1942, followed the next month by General Wainwright's garrison on Corregidor. Other American possessions, such as Guam in the Marianas and Wake Island, were captured in the Japanese juggernaut in December. The Dutch (Netherlands) East Indies also fell to Japanese forces in their drive towards the Southwest Pacific and Indian Ocean. Rabaul on New Britain Island in the Bismarck Archipelago was invaded in February 1942 with the Australian forces there having retreated or been captured. Rabaul, at New Britain's north-eastern tip, became the main bastion for the IJA and IJN in the Southwest Pacific. Japanese outposts were established in Northwest New Guinea and along the northern coast of Papua. Port Moresby on the southern Papuan coast and north-west Australia were now threatened. The massive extent of the Japanese conquest throughout the first half of 1942 was startling. In early June 1942, the USN won a decisive carrier-based aircraft victory over the IJN at the Battle of Midway, thereby eliminating a potential threat to the Hawaiian Islands. *(Meridian Mapping)*

17th Bombardment Group from the flight decks of the USS *Hornet* and *Enterprise* to attack Tokyo (the 'Doolittle Raid'). Although little damage was done, the air-raid solidified the Imperial High Command's approval of Admiral Isoroku Yamamoto's plan to assault Midway Island in June 1942 with the intent of drawing the remnants of Admiral Chester W. Nimitz's US Pacific Fleet into a decisive surface engagement.

However, during the first week of May, USN and IJN task forces duelled with carrier-based aircraft in the Battle of the Coral Sea. A Japanese amphibious invasion of Port Moresby, New Guinea on Papua's southern coast as a possible stepping-stone to invade Australia's Northern Territories was thwarted. The Battle of Midway from 4 to 7 June, another solely carrier-based aircraft clash, ended with a decisive victory for Rear Admiral Raymond A. Spruance's task forces. With the sinking of four IJN carriers under the command of Admiral Chūichi Nagumo, who led the victorious Pearl Harbor attack of 7 December 1941, Imperial Japan's high tide began to ebb.

Coincident with the Coral Sea naval battle in early May 1942, the IJN established a seaplane base on Tulagi, a tiny island in the Florida group across the Sealark Channel from Guadalcanal in the southern Solomon Islands (see Map 2). Tulagi's seizure was part of a larger Japanese military plan for further south-eastward strategic moves against New Caledonia, the New Hebrides, Fiji and Tonga Islands, with its IJN 8th Fleet (the Outer South Seas Force under Vice Admiral Gunichi Mikawa) to eventually close the sea lanes from the United States to the Antipodes' Allied counteroffensive staging areas. USN Admiral Ernest J. King, Commander-in-Chief (C-in-C) and Chief of Naval Operations (CNO), marshalled his forces to interdict the enemy's south-eastward expansion, after a local coast-watcher, District Officer Martin Clemens (a captain commissioned in the British Army), discovered that a Japanese airfield construction party had landed on Guadalcanal on 28 May. On 7 August, the bulk of the US 1st Marine Division (Reinforced), under the command of Major General Alexander A. Vandegrift, amphibiously landed on Guadalcanal, while other Marine speciality units quickly seized Tulagi and Gavutu-Tanambogo. Along Guadalcanal's northern coast, a six-month gruelling Marine defence of the nearly-completed enemy airfield's perimeter (captured and renamed Henderson Field) ensued amid near-constant Japanese aerial and naval bombardment, deadly surface ship action in Sealark Channel (now called 'Iron Bottom Sound'), and sporadic, major IJA ground assaults. The US Army's Americal and 25th Divisions arrived to assist the Marines as reinforcements and eventually moved westward against remaining enemy strongpoints throughout jungles and over mountains. By the first week of February 1943, Japan evacuated Guadalcanal, ending their south-eastern Pacific strategy to isolate the Antipodes.

Early Combat in the Southwest Pacific Area Theatre

On 21 February 1942, President Franklin Roosevelt cabled General Douglas MacArthur, commander of United States Army Forces in the Far East (USAFFE), on Corregidor and ordered him to leave for Australia. After having initially been transported from Corregidor to Mindanao in patrol torpedo (PT) boats, MacArthur and his retinue arrived at Batchelor Field, south of Darwin, on 17 March, in a fleet of battle-weary four-engined B-17 Flying Fortress bombers.

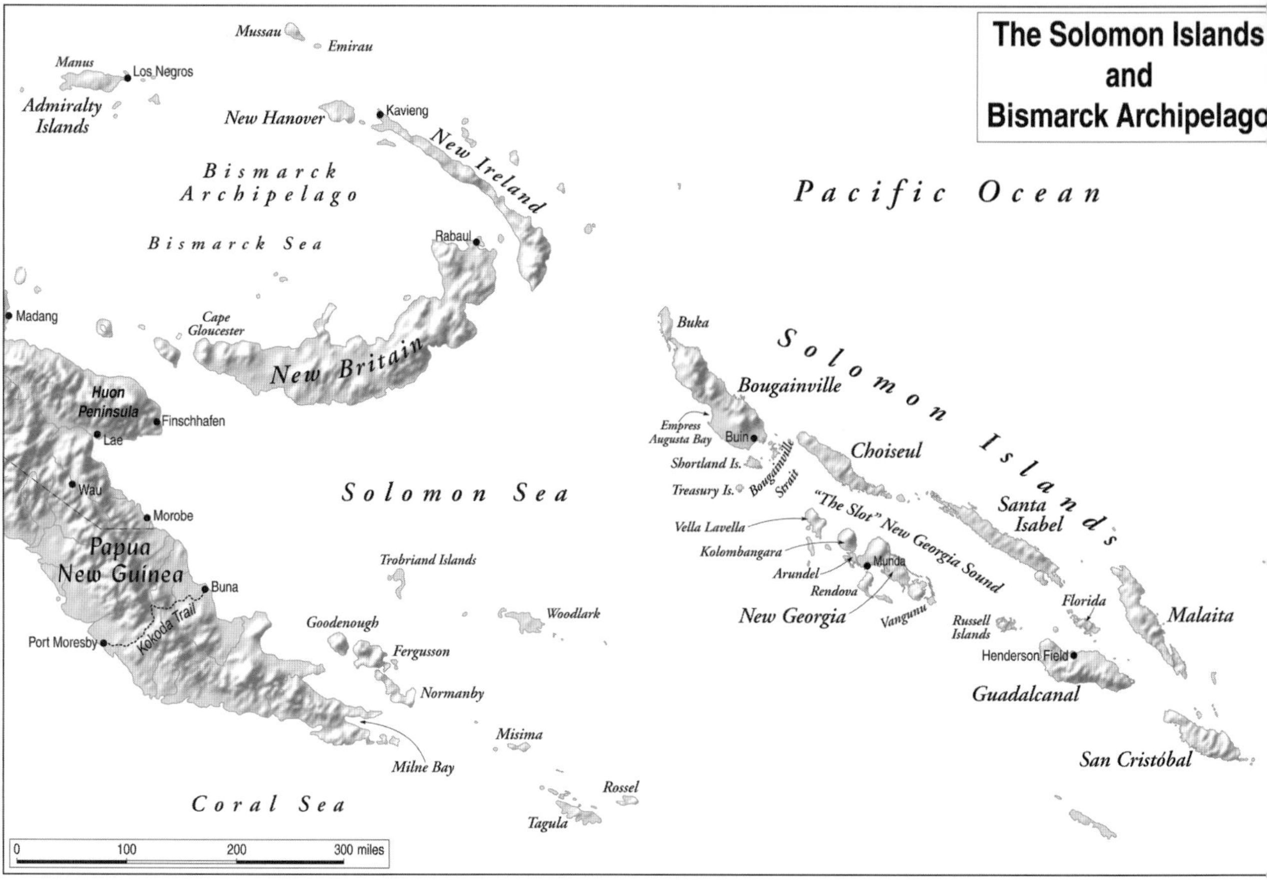

Map 2. The Solomon Islands and Bismarck Archipelago in the South and Southwestern Pacific Areas of Operation, 1942–1943. In order to gain control over the sea lanes in the south-eastern Pacific area and isolate the Antipodes, the IJN occupied and built a seaplane base on the islet of Tulagi off Florida Island in the southern Solomon Islands in early May 1942. Then Japanese engineers and labourers began construction of an airfield along Lunga Plain on the larger island of Guadalcanal (to be renamed by the USMC as Henderson Field). The Japanese expanded their presence from Northeast New Guinea's Huon Peninsula's locales of Lae and Finschhafen by establishing bases along Papua's northern coast, notably at Buna during the late spring of 1942. With the exceptions of Japan's lost or stalemated battles at the Coral Sea (May 1942), Midway (June 1942), Milne Bay (August–September 1942), the overland Buna-to-Port Moresby assault along the Kokoda Trail (July–September 1942) and the failure to quickly defeat an isolated US 1st Marine Division (Reinforced) after the initial Allied naval defeat in Guadalcanal's offshore waters (August 1942), almost all of Japan's initial strategic goals were achieved.

The dual set of Japanese campaigns in Papua and on Guadalcanal across the Solomon Sea during late 1942-early 1943 were to detract strength from one another, posing both tactical and strategic dilemmas for Japan from which she never recovered. The Allies designated the Papua and Northeast New Guinea campaigns to be under General Douglas MacArthur's SWPA. The series of USMC and US Army amphibious assaults up the Solomon Island chain in the New Georgia Island group (July 1943) and at Bougainville (November 1943) were in Vice Admiral William Halsey's SPA. These Allied campaigns created a double envelopment of Rabaul at the north-eastern tip of New Britain Island in the Bismarck Archipelago. Rabaul was not directly invaded but rather neutralized after Japan's loss of air superiority enabled Operation CARTWHEEL's ever-increasing number of Allied land and carrier-based air attacks to isolate the enemy's New Britain bastion. *(Meridian Mapping)*

After seizing Rabaul on New Britain in late January 1942, the IJA and IJN landed units at Salamaua, Lae and Finschhafen on the Huon Gulf in Northeast New Guinea from 8 March to 7 April (see Map 2). In mid-July, Japanese Special Naval Landing Force (SNLF) troops landed at Buna, Gona and Sanananda, along the northern coast of Papua, the eastern third of New Guinea.

In June 1942, MacArthur, now as C-in-C of the Southwest Pacific Area (SWPA), dispatched additional 'green' Australian Militia units to Port Moresby as the US 32nd and 41st Infantry divisions (both American National Guard units) arrived in Australia. The Australian Militia's 39th Battalion, already deployed at Port Moresby, was ordered north to defend Kokoda, which was attacked by the Japanese on 29 July. Eventually reinforced by Middle East veteran Australian Imperial Force (AIF) formations, the Australians combated IJA units across the Owen Stanley Range via the Kokoda Trail as the Japanese tried an overland route to seize Port Moresby. By mid-September 1942, a stiffening Australian defence and orders for the Japanese advance to cease saved Port Moresby again. Also, a second amphibious Japanese invasion at Milne Bay during late August-early September aimed at seizing Port Moresby was turned back by Australian ground and air forces. Now, it was to become the Americans and Australians turn to begin their offensive up the Kokoda Trail and through the Papuan jungle to drive the Japanese from Buna, Gona and Sanananda.

On 10 September 1942, MacArthur ordered Lieutenant General Robert L. Eichelberger's I Corps headquarters (HQ) to deploy Major General Edwin Harding's 32nd Infantry Division to capture the 11-mile-long group of Japanese installations at Buna. After a few months of arduous marching and combat against a bunkered Japanese foe, the unprepared American former National Guardsmen, with the aid of battle-hardened Australians, evicted the Japanese from their installations by January 1943. However, a steep Allied 'butcher bill' was incurred and MacArthur vowed, 'No more Bunas.'

After the bittersweet successes of Guadalcanal and Papua, three separate axes of Allied advances were conducted in the SWPA, South and Central Pacific areas. Beginning in January 1943, MacArthur's Australian-American forces seized strategic locales along the Northwest New Guinea's northern coast and among nearby islands (e.g. Woodlark, Kiriwina, Goodenough) in the Solomon Sea as well as at the southern end of New Britain (Cape Gloucester and Arawe), while bypassing Japanese strongholds. Strategically, the Allies seized extant enemy airfields or built new ones for future Allied aerial operations to neutralize Rabaul by air (see Map 2).

Action in the South Pacific Area After Guadalcanal (see Map 3)

In the South Pacific Area (SPA), Admiral (promoted 18 November 1942) Halsey's forces of Marines and Army troops quickly occupied and constructed airfields in the Russell Islands (Pavuvu the largest one) in late February 1943. Then, the war in the

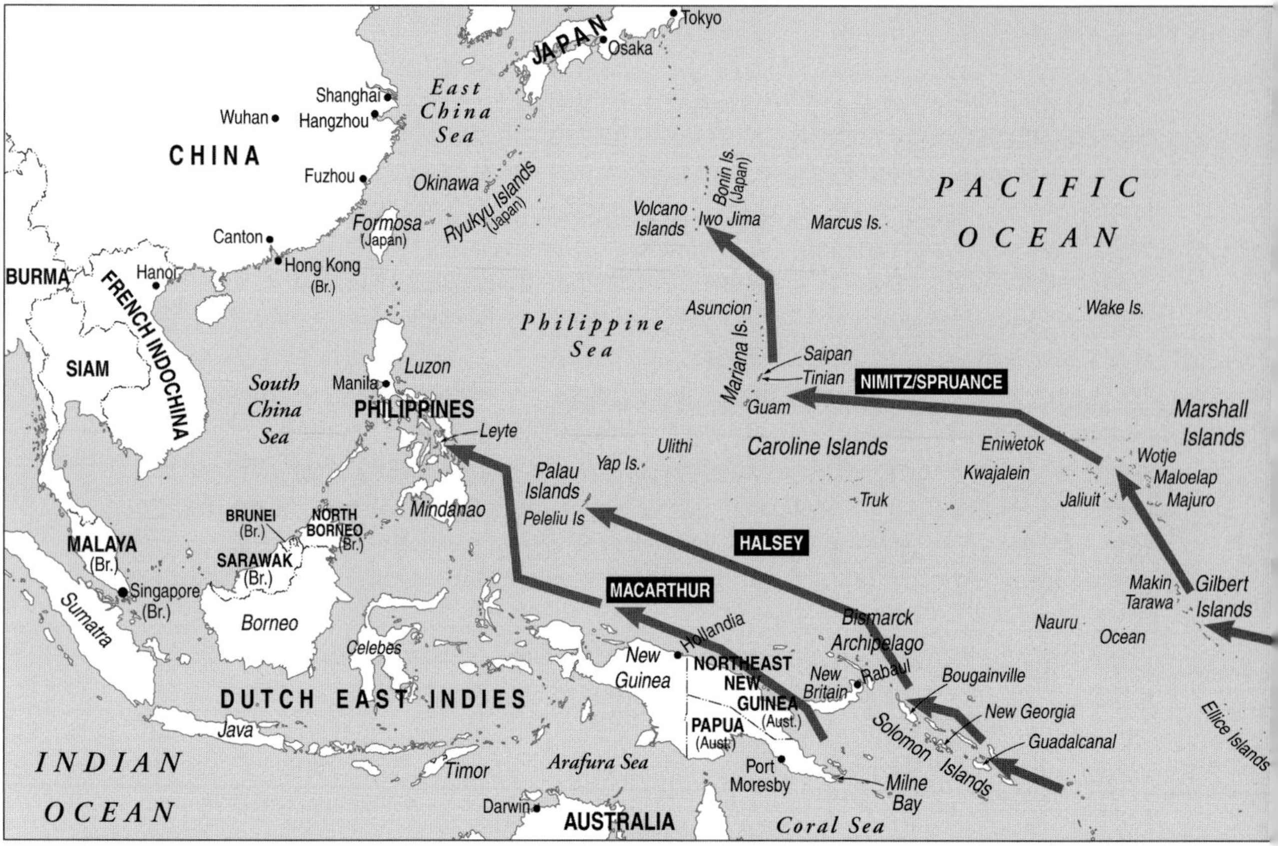

Map 3. Allied Counteroffensive Axes in the Central, South and Southwest Pacific Areas of Operation, 1943–1944. In early 1943, three Allied axes of advance developed. In the CPA, Admiral Nimitz assigned, in August 1943, his COS Vice Admiral Raymond Spruance to command the Central Pacific Force (later re-designated Fifth Fleet in April 1944). This USN, Marine and Army force advanced on separate invasions and hotly contested campaigns in the Gilbert Islands (November 1943), the Marshall Islands (January–February 1944) and the Marianas (June–August 1944). After the seizure of the Marianas, Nimitz and Spruance's staffs were drawing up plans to ultimately seize Iwo Jima in the Volcano Islands south of the Bonin Island chain and to the north-west of Saipan. As the Allied Pacific drives were rapidly moving westward, the IJN naval bastion of Truk in the eastern Caroline Islands was bypassed.

In the SPA, Vice Admiral William Halsey commanded his Third Fleet up the Solomon Islands with contentious island combat in the New Georgia group (July–September 1943) and Bougainville (November 1943).

In the SWPA, General Douglas MacArthur with his Australian and American ground forces and US Navy's Seventh Fleet vessels drove up the northern coast of Northeast and Dutch New Guinea (1943–44). The southern end of New Britain was invaded by Marine and US Army amphibious forces in December 1943, while Rabaul was neutralized in an aerial campaign, Operation CARTWHEEL. MacArthur's ultimate goal was to invade and return to the Philippines in the latter half of 1944. Halsey's role was unclear after the Solomon Islands and Bismarck Archipelago had been either seized or neutralized. As events were to unfold, MacArthur's Sixth Army landed at Leyte on 20 October 1944 and Halsey was tasked to protect the SWPA commander's 'right flank' by seizing Peleliu, Angaur and Ulithi Atoll in the Palau group of the Western Caroline Islands. *(Meridian Mapping)*

South Pacific continued with the invasion of the Japanese-defended New Georgia group of islands in the Central Solomons in early July. After several weeks of combat involving Marine Raider Battalions and US Army XIVth Corps divisions (37th, 43rd and 25th) against a stubborn and suicidal Japanese defence, primarily centred at Munda Airfield on New Georgia Island, the Japanese bastion was conquered. Amphibious operations under Halsey's leadership continued against other Japanese-occupied islands in the Central Solomons group: Arundel, Vella Lavella, Choiseul and the Treasuries.

These amphibious assaults served as a prelude to the invasion of the heavily-defended and largest Solomon Island, Bougainville, along Cape Torokina at Empress Augusta Bay on 1 November 1943. I Marine Amphibious Corps (IMAC), initially commanded by Marine Lieutenant General Vandegrift followed by Major General Roy S. Geiger, comprised the 3rd Marine Division as well as Marine Raider and Defence battalions. MacArthur, the SWPA theatre commander, wanted Halsey's aircraft established on newly-constructed airfields at Cape Torokina within fighter range of Rabaul, the latter at the northern end of New Britain Island. Halsey's aircraft on Bougainville were needed in a timely fashion to assist with the aerial neutralization of that Japanese bastion (Operation CARTWHEEL), as well as to help provide air cover for the US Army's 112th Cavalry Regiment and the 1st Marine Division's invasions at Arawe and Cape Gloucester at New Britain's southern end on 15 and 26 December respectively.

Soon to follow IMAC was the US Army's XIV Corps (37th and Americal Divisions), under Major General Oscar. W. Griswold (who turned the tide earlier at New Georgia). XIV Corps enlarged and fortified the Cape Torokina perimeter, built new airfields, and awaited a massive IJA 17th Army counterattack (to be launched in early March 1944), which was successfully defeated by the American soldiers.

Amphibious Island Assaults in the Central Pacific Area (see Map 3)

The Central Pacific Area (CPA) of operations was under the overall command of Admiral Chester W. Nimitz, who was also C-in-C, Pacific Ocean Area (CINPOA). Under Nimitz was Vice Admiral Raymond A. Spruance, the naval victor at Midway and now the US Fifth Fleet commander. Under their leadership, the 2nd Marine Division, along with elements of the US Army's 27th Division, comprised V Amphibious Corps (VAC, 35,000 troops). This force invaded the Gilbert Islands' Tarawa and Makin Atolls, respectively, the first major American offensive in this oceanic sector by the US Fifth Fleet. After hellacious combat from 20 to 23 November 1943 on mainly Betio Island in the south-west of Tarawa Atoll, against 4,500 suicidal and entrenched 7th Sasebo SNLF and 3rd Special Base Defence troops, this Gilbert group of islands and its airfields were seized at a steep price in American bloodshed (approximately 1,700 killed and 2,100 wounded). During the same time period, at Makin Atoll, principally on Butaritari Island, the 27th Division's 165th Infantry Regiment eliminated the small Japanese garrison's fortified positions one at a time. The USS *Liscome Bay*, an escort carrier, was sunk (644 sailors lost) by a Japanese submarine and the battleship USS *Mississippi* damaged with a turret fire (more than 40 seamen killed).

The Marshall Islands, a series of oceanic atolls, ceded to Japan at the end of the First World War, had numerous enemy airfields as well as seaplane and naval bases. More than 25,000 IJA and IJN troops awaited Nimitz's next CPA move after the Gilbert Islands combat. Majuro Atoll (in the Marshall Islands' south-eastern sector) was initially occupied against limited enemy resistance by a reconnaissance company of Marines from VAC along with a battalion of the US 27th Division's 106th Infantry Regiment (IR) on 30 January 1944. The next day, the USN Fifth Fleet's (under Spruance) carrier aircraft attacked Japanese airfields on Kwajalein Atoll's islands. Roi-Namur Islands, the northernmost within Kwajalein Atoll, were attacked by the 4th Marine Division, while Kwajalein Island, at the atoll's south-eastern atoll tip, was invaded by the US 7th Infantry Division on 31 January. Roi was secured on 1 February with Namur successfully occupied the next day. It was not until 4 February that Kwajalein Island was secured. The amphibious assault on Eniwetok Atoll began on 19 February with the separate 22nd Marines and elements of the US 27th Division's 106th IR attacking. The entire island was secured two days later. Eniwetok Atoll's airfields and anchorages were to become the major staging areas for Nimitz's next CPA expedition, the Mariana Islands.

US Army and Marine forces invaded Saipan on 15 June 1944 and secured it after heavy fighting on 9 July. The IJN response to the US Fifth Fleet's presence resulted in the carrier aircraft clash on 19–20 June, the Battle of the Philippine Sea (the 'Great Marianas Turkey Shoot'), destroying IJN aerial capacity (480 planes and 3 large carriers). When IJN Admiral Ozawa reached Okinawa after the battle, he had only thirty-five serviceable carrier planes. Guam and Tinian, the other large islands in the Marianas, were invaded on 21 July and 24 July respectively, and secured. Saipan and Tinian were to become major air bases for US B-29 Superfortress bombing of Japan's Home Islands.

MacArthur's SWPA 1943–44 New Guinea Campaign

The Japanese built up the prewar airfield and harbour at Lae in Northeast New Guinea into a major base and anchorage on the Huon Peninsula. Japanese planners proposed an advance from Lae onto Wau with the intent of yet another attack on Port Moresby along a different geographic axis than via the Kokoda Trail. However, the Allied air forces prevented Japanese reinforcements from landing at Lae and a combined Allied offensive was launched during the summer of 1943 to capture the enemy bastion.

Elements of the US 41st Infantry Division pushed along the coast, while the Australians advanced on a western axis from Wau through the Markham Valley. The Australians continued in the Allied offensive on the Huon Peninsula at Lae, Salamaua, Finschhafen, and in the Markham River Valley. Here, the terrain and climate were daunting, as well as this area being rife with tropical diseases.

Japanese losses in their prolonged defence of Salamaua against the American and Australian advance left Lae exposed to an Allied envelopment. On 4 September 1943, almost 8,000 troops of the 7th Australian Division landed 18 miles east of Lae in the rear of Japanese defences, the first step in General Sir Thomas Blamey's New Guinea Force to clear the Huon Peninsula. After capturing Lae, the 7th Australian Division advanced west into the upper Ramu Valley to secure airfields for Lieutenant General George Kenney's US Fifth Air Force. The 9th Australian Division landed near Finschhafen and, against strong opposition at Sattelberg, these veteran troops eventually cleared the western shore of the Vitiaz Strait.

Throughout the earlier part of 1944, MacArthur's SWPA ground forces, comprising the US Sixth Army's (under Lieutenant General Walter Krueger) 6th, 24th, 32nd and 41st Infantry divisions, with attached elite cavalry, parachute, engineer and scout units, along with the 1st Marine Division given to MacArthur for the campaign on southern New Britain Island, were transported by the growing VII Amphibious Force (under Rear Admiral Daniel Barbey) of the US Seventh Fleet. These SWPA ground forces moved inexorably westward along the northern coast of Netherlands New Guinea and New Britain's Willaumez Peninsula with successful missions at Saidor (2 January), the Admiralty Islands (29 February), Talasea (6 March), Aitape (22 April), Hollandia (22 April), Tanahmerah Bay (22 April), Wakde Island (18 May), Biak Island at the entrance of Geelvink Bay (27 May), Middelburg Island (30 June), Sansapor on the Vogelkop Peninsula (30 June), and Noemfoor Island (2 July).

Background to the Palau Islands Campaign

At the November 1943 Cairo Conference, Allied war leaders recognized that ultimate aims of the American Pacific offensives included the Philippines' liberation, a Formosa invasion and establishing East China coastal air bases during late 1944 into spring of 1945 (see Map 4). However, with Allied Pacific victories accumulating throughout mid-1943, MacArthur persuaded Roosevelt and the JCS at Pearl Harbor in July that repossessing the Philippines would sever Imperial Japan's conquests in two and solidify the SWPA commander's promise of 'I Shall Return' to the Filipino citizenry. Enthusiasm for Nimitz's CPA fleet invading Formosa and possibly seizing East China coast air bases dissipated, although an invasion of the Ryuku Islands prior to the Japanese Home Islands would fall in the CPA's domain.

In order to protect MacArthur's flanks for a proposed Mindanao invasion, two other amphibious operations were required. First, Morotai in the in the Halmahera

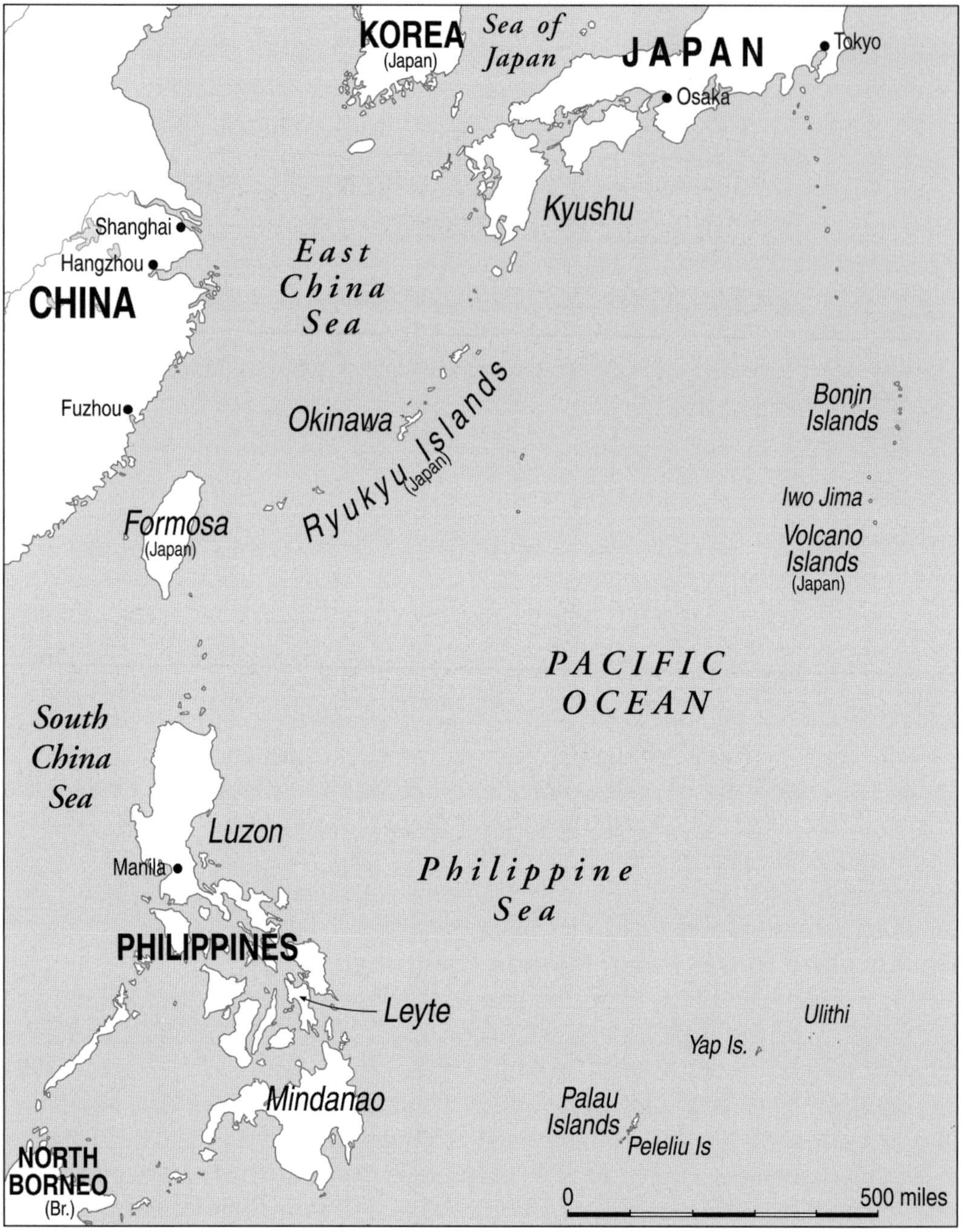

Map 4. Convergence of Allied Pacific Counteroffensives, 1944. At the Allied Cairo Conference in November 1943, the proposed aims of the American Pacific offensives included the liberation of the Philippines, a Formosa invasion and establishing air bases along the East China coast during late 1944 into the spring of 1945. Nimitz expressed his desire to invade the Japanese-controlled island of Formosa and, perhaps, seize East China coast bases as a prelude to a CPA advance on the

group of the eastern NEI's Molucca chain, situated 300 miles from the Philippines, would cover MacArthur's 'left flank', and was to be assaulted by the US Army's 31st Infantry Division and some Australian forces on 15 September. Neutralizing the Palau Islands was deemed necessary to secure MacArthur's 'right flank'. American intelligence was aware that at the start of the Pacific War, Palau-based IJA planes struck the southern Philippines. Peleliu's airfield was only 500 miles west of Mindanao. Also, in the closing weeks of December 1941, Palau-based Japanese troops invaded the central and southern Philippine Islands. Thus, the US 1st Marine and 81st Army divisions were to assault Peleliu and Angaur Islands within the Palau Group commencing on 15 September 1944 to prevent Japanese aerial interdiction of MacArthur's attack on Mindanao.

After the First World War, the League of Nations mandated the islands north of the equator to Japan. The Palau island of Koror (see Map 5) was extensively built up by the Japanese with docking and harbour facilities, paved main roads and permanent concrete buildings. Some modernization was brought to Angaur, the southern-most of the Palau Islands, as the Japanese sought to harvest the rich phosphate

---

Ryuku Islands and then Japan's Home Islands. With this CPA offensive, the Philippines would be bypassed.

At a conference at Pearl Harbor on 26 July 1944 between Roosevelt, MacArthur, Nimitz and Admiral William Leahy, the above plans were modified. MacArthur persuaded Roosevelt and the JCS that returning to the Philippines would sever Japan's conquests in two and enable the SWPA commander to honour his promise of 'I Shall Return' to the Filipino citizenry. The American Joint Chiefs of Staff (JCS) instructed MacArthur's SWPA forces to liberate the Philippine Archipelago, beginning with the southern island of Mindanao, after focus shifted away from an invasion of Formosa. In order to protect MacArthur's flanks, two other amphibious operations were required. First, Morotai in the Moluccas, situated 300 miles from the Philippines, which comprised MacArthur's 'left flank', was to be assaulted by the US Army's 31st Infantry Division and some Australian forces. To secure MacArthur's 'right flank', Halsey's Third Fleet was to attack Peleliu and Angaur in the Palau group of the western Caroline Islands, directly due east of Mindanao, in September. Nimitz decided not to attack well-defended Yap Island to the north-east of the Palau Islands, but planned on assaulting Ulithi Atoll, further to the north-east in the Caroline Islands, with an 81st Division IR to obtain a favourable fleet anchorage site.

After the seizure of the Marianas, Nimitz ordered Spruance's Fifth Fleet staff to draw up plans to seize Iwo Jima, located in the Volcano Islands just to the south of the Bonin Island chain and to Japan's south-east and the Mariana Islands' north-west. Iwo Jima was a heavily-fortified island with two well-constructed air bases, which enabled Japanese fighter squadrons to interdict the advancing American LOC further westward across the CPA towards the East China Sea. Also, once captured, these airfields could base P-51 fighter escorts to accompany the Mariana-based B-29 Superfortress bombers that were suffering heavy losses on their 2,500-mile round trip over Japanese cities and military targets. Iwo Jima's airfields were also envisioned as emergency landing sites for damaged B-29 Superfortress bombers on their return leg from the Japanese Home Islands to their Mariana Islands bases.

American commanders were also planning an assault on Okinawa in the Ryuku Islands as a prelude to and staging area for the final invasion of the Japanese Home Islands. *(Meridian Mapping)*

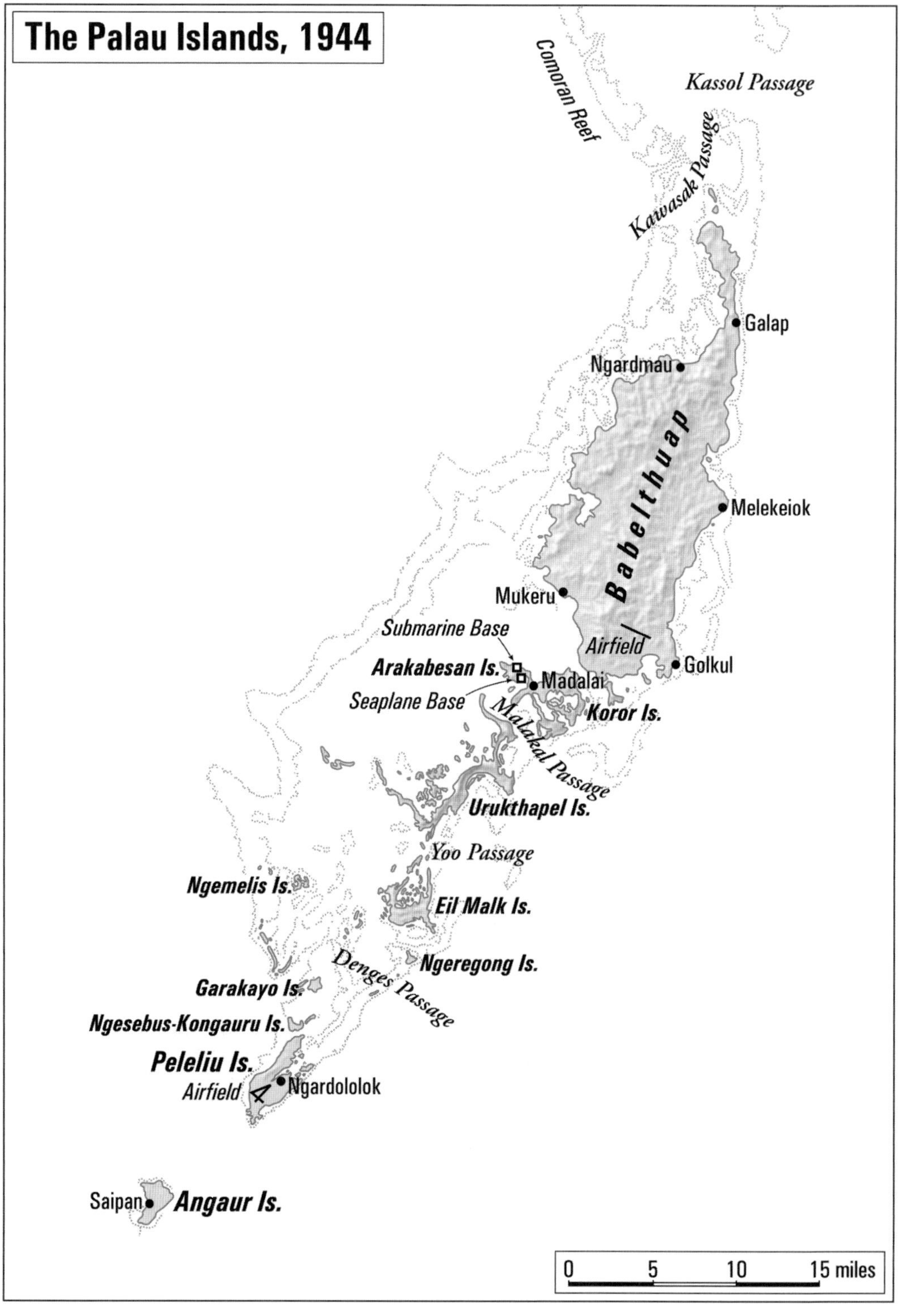
The Palau Islands, 1944
Comoran Reef
Kassol Passage
Kawasak Passage
Galap
Ngardmau
Babelthuap
Melekeiok
Mukeru
Submarine Base
Airfield
Golkul
Arakabesan Is.
Madalai
Seaplane Base
Malakal Passage
Koror Is.
Urukthapel Is.
Yoo Passage
Ngemelis Is.
Eil Malk Is.
Ngeregong Is.
Denges Passage
Garakayo Is.
Ngesebus-Kongauru Is.
Peleliu Is.
Airfield
Ngardololok
Saipan
Angaur Is.
0 5 10 15 miles

deposits. Additional phosphate deposits were found on Peleliu and the Japanese built a refinery there, which was abandoned before the American invasion in September 1944.

The major construction by the Japanese in the Palau Islands was a two-runway airstrip on the southern end of Peleliu, completed in 1938 and undergoing improvement. This airfield was a major reason for the US landing at Peleliu and Angaur. A new one was constructed on Babelthuap, the largest of the Palau Islands. These airfields were of major importance to the Americans with MacArthur's planned invasion of Mindanao. The Japanese defeats of 1943–44 forced Tokyo to reconsider the Palau Islands in the Western Carolines as a new second line of defence. Defensive fortifications in the Palau Islands were to be constructed in which Japanese troops, using their *Bushido* code, were to fight without surrender.

In February–March 1944, US carrier planes from Admiral Marc Mitscher's Task Force 58 attacked Koror, Babelthuap, Peleliu and Ngesebus (just to Peleliu's north), the latter with an airfield under construction. IJN surface ships at Koror's anchorage were sunk or damaged in these raids. Ironically, Nimitz's fleet now controlled the air and sea lanes to the Palau Islands with the admiral noting that 'MacArthur's right flank was safe', well before a decision was made to seize Peleliu, Angaur and Ulithi. If it

---

Map 5. The Palau Islands, 1944. The Palau Islands are shown running in a north-easterly direction from Angaur Island in the extreme south to the largest island, Babelthuap. The major airfield construction by the Japanese in the Palau Islands was a two-runway airstrip completed in 1938 on the southern end of Peleliu. This airfield had been improved since its completion and was a major reason for the American invasion of Peleliu. The largest island of Babelthuap also had a newer single-runway airfield on that island's southern end. There were seaplane facilities on Koror and Arakabesan Islands, the latter two in the middle of the Palau group just to the south of Babelthuap.

The Palau Islands' airfields were of major importance to the Americans with MacArthur's upcoming planned invasion of Mindanao by the SWPA's amphibious forces. Japanese bombers, based in the Palau Islands, participated in the attack on the Philippines on the first day of the Pacific War. Within the next two weeks, Japanese troops from the Palaus invaded the central and southern Philippine Islands. Neutralizing the Palau Islands was deemed necessary to secure MacArthur's 'right flank'. However, in February–March 1944, US carrier planes from Admiral Marc Mitscher's Task Force 58 attacked Koror, Babelthuap, Peleliu and Ngesebus, the latter with an airfield under construction. IJN surface ships at Koror's anchorage were also sunk or severely damaged in these raids.

Lieutenant General Sadae Inoue, now in charge of the Palau Sector Group, established his HQ with his 14th Division on Koror after the IJN relinquished command there along with all other forces in the Palaus. His total garrison strength in the Palau Islands was 35,000 troops. With Babelthuap suspected as the next American invasion site, Inoue stationed approximately 25,000 of them including the bulk of the IJA 15th and 59th IRs. Peleliu, with its important airfield, was only defended by the IJA 2nd IR reinforced with a battalion of the 15th IR, an infantry battalion of the 53rd Independent Mixed Brigade, along with naval and other troops totalling 10,500 men. Angaur had a reinforced battalion (1,500 men) of the IJA 59th IR. All of these Japanese ground forces lacked air and naval support since the USN carrier strikes of February–March 1944 destroyed practically all Peleliu-based aircraft and the IJN had moved westward to safer anchorages. *(Meridian Mapping)*

were not for a lingering fear of Japanese aircraft from Peleliu interfering with SWPA forces landing on Mindanao, then the entire Palau group might have been bypassed, as was the IJN bastion on Truk in the eastern Carolines.

Halsey's USN Third Fleet staff and that of the Joint Expeditionary Force of the 1st Marine Division and the Army's 81st Infantry Division troops, comprising III Amphibious Corps (IIIAC), was delegated by Nimitz in early April 1944 with the operational planning of an upcoming Palau Islands campaign. The target date for the invasion of Peleliu and Angaur was scheduled for 15 September. Originally, during early planning, the US Army's XXIV Corps was tentatively assigned with the more challenging Operation STALEMATE to seize the largest Palau Group island of Babelthuap on 8 September. However, Nimitz cancelled STALEMATE on 7 July due to protracted fighting on Saipan and Guam in the Mariana Islands and the continued commitment of those Army troops there throughout June–August 1944. Feasibility studies also showed that the heavily-garrisoned Babelthuap was going to be difficult to invade. A revised Operation STALEMATE II now abandoned securing Babelthuap and substituted Ulithi and Yap Atolls while keeping the attacks on Peleliu and Angaur as planned with Peleliu's airfield being the prime objective. Ulithi Atoll, to the north-east of the Palau group, was to be assaulted by an 81st Division IR in order to obtain suitable anchorages for the massive USN fleet.

Admiral Halsey, who was previously the joint commander of the SPA and was now in charge of the Third Fleet's operations in the CPA, had reservations that an assault on the heavily-defended Palaus was likely to be a bloodbath, despite securing the airfields and anchorages there. The Palaus were reinforced with the IJA 14th Division, veterans from the IJA's Kwantung Army in Manchuria, which was sent to Koror in mid-April 1944, augmenting that island group's garrison's strength to 35,000 troops.

US aerial reconnaissance, during the initial few days of September 1944, showed that the Japanese airfields at Peleliu and Babelthuap had not been completely repaired after the USN Task Force 58's carrier strikes of March 1944. Also, the number of Japanese bombers in the Palau group was probably not a significant force and therefore could have been dealt with by further USN carrier strikes. Furthermore, during carrier-based air-raids over Mindanao and the central Philippines, American Intelligence observed a weakness of Japanese air power there that had led Halsey to publicly question the direction of the projected invasions and timetable for the Philippine operation. On 13 September, Halsey's staff sent an urgent message to Nimitz that recommended that the seizure of the Palaus and Yap be abandoned, as well as transferring the troops for those operations to MacArthur for a Philippine invasion. Also, Halsey suggested that the assault on Leyte be undertaken as soon as possible due to the weakness of Japanese air forces in the southern and central Philippines.

It was Nimitz's decision that the invasions of Peleliu and Angaur were still to be undertaken, while Ulithi Atoll and not Yap Atoll was also to be assaulted. Nimitz never explained fully his rationale to overrule Halsey's suggestions except noting that the 1st Marine and 81st Infantry divisions were already at sea and that the commitment to the operation up till then negated calling off the invasion of the Palaus. In the end, Nimitz hoped to acquire, without much bloodshed, permanent bases with airfields in the Palau group that could support SWPA operations in the Philippines as well as further advances in the CPA towards Iwo Jima and Okinawa in the Volcano and Ryuku Islands respectively. The invasion of the Palau Islands, Operation STALEMATE II, was set for 15 September after the capture of Saipan, Guam and Tinian in the Marianas during June-August.

A Japanese patrol is seen charging through the streets of a Chinese town after large swathes of China were seized with numerous atrocities committed against the civilian population during many years of war on the Asian mainland prior to the December 1941 series of attacks and invasions across the Pacific. (*NARA*)

A column of IJA tankettes is shown manoeuvring through a village lane in China during the Sino-Japanese War, which officially started in early July 1937 following the 'Marco Polo Bridge Incident'. These lightly-armoured tankettes, successful in China, were wholly inadequate against American armoured vehicles landing on Japanese-defended islands across the Pacific like Peleliu. *(NARA)*

Two Japanese soldiers are shown leading a camel through a cultivated field in the Chinese interior during the Sino-Japanese War. Although not specifically trained for the various climates and terrains in which the IJA would campaign, Japanese soldiers quickly adapted, which was advantageous against less resilient enemies. *(NARA)*

An IJN bomber is shown taking off from the carrier *Shokaku*, one of six that participated in Admiral Chūichi Nagumo's surprise attack on Pearl Harbor and other US military installations and civilian sites on Oahu on 7 December 1941. Among many USN vessels attacked, four battleships were sunk and another four damaged. More than 2,400 Americans perished in the attack, with in excess of 1,000 wounded. The Japanese lost twenty-nine aircraft during the two waves of aerial assault. *(NARA)*

Two IJN airmen are shown unloading bombs from a truck at a French Indochinese airfield for an attack on the Royal Navy battleship HMS *Prince of Wales* and the battlecruiser HMS *Repulse*, which comprised the major surface vessels of Admiral Sir Tom Phillips' Force Z. The IJN aerial attack occurred on 10 December 1941 off the east coast of Malaya near Kuantan in the South China Sea. More than 800 RN sailors died in the assault and the British Eastern Fleet based in Singapore was severely weakened. Eighty-eight IJN Mitsubishi G4M (Betty) and G3M (Nell) twin-engined, medium land-based horizontal and torpedo-bombers of the Genzan, Kanoya and Mihoro Air Groups participated in the devastating attack during the latter part of Force Z's failed attempt to halt the Japanese amphibious landings near Kota Bharu, Malaya that started on 8 December. Captain William Tennant of the *Repulse*, a major RN supervisor at Dunkirk during the evacuation in late May to early June 1940, survived and was rescued by an escorting destroyer after abandoning his sinking vessel. The escorting destroyers managed to save more than 2,000 of the almost 3,000 crewmen of the two destroyed RN capital vessels. Admiral Phillips, the Force Z commander, and Captain John Leach commanding the *Prince of Wales*, both died with their ship's sinking. Four Japanese aircraft were destroyed and another twenty-eight damaged by AA fire from the Force Z guns. *(NARA)*

(**Opposite, above**) USAAF planes lay destroyed after the Japanese attack on Oahu's Wheeler Field, the Army's main fighter base. More than 185 US aircraft in total were destroyed and another 155 damaged on the ground at Wheeler (above), Hickam, and Bellows Fields as well as Kaneohe, Ford Island, and Barbers Point Naval Air Stations. In addition, the Marine Corps Air Station Ewa, 7 miles west of Pearl Harbor, was the first US military installation hit during the attack. All of Ewa's forty-eight aircraft were destroyed on the ground. *(NARA)*

(**Opposite, below**) An Australian 2-pounder AT gun is shown ambushing a column of Type 95 *Ke-Go* light Japanese tanks on the Muar-Bakri Road in Malaya's Johore Province in early 1942. British and Commonwealth forces lacked their own armour since in pre-war planning it was believed that the Malayan jungle would be impenetrable to tanks. *(NARA)*

Victorious IJA 25th Army soldiers are shown humiliating British and Commonwealth infantrymen by making them raise their arms for cameramen while surrendering in Singapore City on 15 February 1942. It was the greatest capitulation of British arms in the Empire's history. Approximately 80,000 British, Indian and Australian troops in Singapore surrendered, in addition to the previous 50,000 that had become prisoners of war during combat on the Malayan Peninsula. *(Author's collection)*

Major General Jonathan Wainwright (left) with General Douglas A. MacArthur are shown here on 10 October 1941. Wainwright was the commander of the North Luzon Force, I Philippine Corps. MacArthur was the commanding general of the United States Army Forces Far East (USAFFE). When MacArthur left for Australia in March 1942, Wainwright succeeded him, only to surrender all American forces on Corregidor on 6 May 1942. *(NARA)*

Filipino workers supervised by a Philippine Scout soldier are shown preparing a partially-destroyed bridge for demolition. MacArthur and his local commanders believed that the Philippines' many rivers would delay a Japanese advance. American war planners in Washington believed that the Philippine Islands were indefensible due to deficient field forces in disparate locales amid differing terrain. By destroying many of the bridges during an American-Filipino retreat, local American leaders believed that Japanese sappers would have to rebuild temporary bridges which might not be adequate for IJA armour. *(NARA)*

(**Above**) A Japanese field gun is shown firing at American-Filipino forces retreating into the Bataan Peninsula on the southern part of Luzon. The IJA relied on its heavy artillery, transported from Malaya and Singapore, to batter American-Filipino positions on Bataan as the IJA 14th Army forces, led by General Masaharu Homma, had already lost almost 3,000 soldiers killed, 4,000 wounded and thousands more made non-combatant by disease. Already behind schedule to capture the Philippines, Homma's heavy artillery was to first break the Orion-Bagac Line on Bataan and with a consequent American-Filipino capitulation, these guns were to be unleashed on Corregidor. *(NARA)*

(**Opposite, above**) A Japanese flame-thrower team is shown attacking an American pillbox on the Orion-Bagac Line in late winter 1942. Although American-Filipino resistance was stout at many defensive sites, the lack of food, ammunition and medical supplies created havoc among the Bataan defenders. *(Author's collection)*

(**Opposite, below**) An American soldier wearing a First World War Brodie-pattern 'doughboy' helmet is shown here in a slit trench holding a 'Molotov cocktail' awaiting a Japanese tank column's advance. Although US light tanks and M3 half-tracks carrying 75mm howitzers of the 192nd TB successfully engaged IJA Type 89 I-Go medium tanks before the retreat into the Bataan Peninsula in late December 1941, American AT capability dwindled due to enemy aerial attacks, leaving infantrymen with only rudimentary means to stop Japanese armour. *(NARA)*

(**Above**) US Army Captain Arthur Wermuth, with a fellow Filipino officer, is shown with their personal weapons. Wermuth reportedly killed more than 100 IJA soldiers in clashes along American-Filipino defensive positions during the retreat to and within the Bataan Peninsula. Ad hoc forces of soldiers, Marines, sailors and airmen delayed General Homma's advance to the chagrin of Tokyo and occasionally captured IJA soldiers too. *(NARA)*

(**Opposite, above**) American PoWs are shown here carrying their dead comrades under Japanese guard for burial outside Camp O'Donnell on Luzon. American and Filipino forces surrendered on 9 April 1942 after a three-month struggle to defend the Bataan Peninsula. The PoWs were brutally led by the Japanese to Camp O'Donnell and other points for incarceration during the hellish 'Bataan Death March'. *(NARA)*

(**Opposite, below**) A Marine sergeant is seen here demonstrating a Lewis gun drum magazine to Filipino soldiers on Corregidor. The Filipino forces on Corregidor, like those on Bataan previously, comprised a variety of ad hoc units that were being trained as infantry to fight the Japanese. *(NARA)*

(**Above**) American troops are shown surrendering as they exit Corregidor's Malinta Tunnel on 6 May 1942. Although the tunnel had four entrances, it possessed numerous lateral passages that had many functions including a headquarters area, storage facilities and a hospital. The tunnel's power plant was disabled by Japanese bombardment causing ventilation and lighting problems until an enemy ground assault on the island fortress caused General Wainwright to surrender the garrison. *(NARA)*

(**Opposite, above**) At Rabaul on New Britain Island in the Bismarck Archipelago, Japanese SNLF troops are shown moving against Australian defensive installations after the South Seas Force entered Simpson Harbour on 23 January 1942. The Japanese invasion quickly overpowered the Australians, many of whom were massacred upon surrendering. Rabaul, with its excellent anchorage at Simpson Harbour, served the IJN vessels while numerous airfields were completed for future offensive operations. *(Author's collection)*

(**Opposite, below**) Japanese infantry with bayonets fixed to their Arisaka rifles are seen rapidly advancing northwards from Rangoon to the outskirts of Mandalay at the end of April 1942. British General Sir Harold Alexander arrived in Burma in early March to stem the Japanese advance, but he was unsuccessful at repeated battle locales. On 26 April, Alexander withdrew as much of his Burma Army as possible to India for reorganization and to defend the subcontinent from a feared Japanese invasion there. *(Author's collection)*

MANDAL

Henderson Field on Guadalcanal's Lunga Plain is shown from a low-flying American airplane. Trees in the coconut plantation (right) were felled to make room for the airfield. Just before the 1st Marine Division invasion on 7 August 1942, the Japanese nearly completed the airstrip with a runway that was over 3,500ft long and 150ft wide. Only the unfinished corner of the runway needed to be levelled and surfaced. District Officer Martin Clemens, a Cambridge graduate and captain commissioned in the British Army, was situated at Aola along the northern coastal plain to the east. On 28 May 1942, Clemens became aware of a Japanese landing party surveying Lunga Plain and forwarded the information to Australia. This was an inspection party of Captain Shigetoshi Miyazaki of the seaplane-equipped Yokohama Air Group stationed at Tulagi across Sealark Channel from Guadalcanal. From June to July 1942, more than 2,500 men of the 11th and 13th Construction Units landed at Lunga Point to build the airfield on Lunga Plain under Clemens' and his scouts' surveillance. *(NARA)*

Elements of IJA Major General Tomitaro Horii's South Seas Detachment are shown receiving orders along the Kokoda Trail. The *Nankai Shitai* was initially composed of the 144th IR and various support units from the IJA 55th Division, including artillery, signals, transport, engineer and medical units. Prior combat experience included landings on Guam in the Mariana Islands and the capture of Rabaul. On 1 July 1942, orders were given to Colonel Yosuke Yokoyama's advance force comprising a battalion of the IJA 144th IR along with the 15th Independent Engineer Regiment, a mountain artillery company and other support units to land on the northern Papuan beaches and to secure an airstrip at Kokoda Village and move as far south as the saddle of the Owen Stanley Range. Some 900 other infantrymen of the 144th IR landed at Gona on 20–21 July from Rabaul. There was no sign of Australian troops at Gona; however, the Japanese convoy in the Gona anchorage was attacked by scores of Australian planes, including P-400 Airacobras, from Port Moresby, the objective of the Japanese overland expedition. To the east, additional landings were made at Buna, which was to be transformed into a base and support centre for the Port Moresby offensive starting on 22 July. *(Author's collection)*

Japanese combat engineers are shown here repairing a bridge across a stream on the Kokoda Trail. More than 2,000 engineers as well as Formosan and Korean labourers worked arduously to keep Japanese LOC open from the Buna and Gona bases to the front line. IJA planners calculated the marching distance from Buna to Port Moresby as 360 kilometres. Thousands of porters were required since there was no vehicular road to assist in bringing supplies and ammunition to the 5,000 soldiers advancing south along the Kokoda Trail towards Port Moresby. *(Author's collection)*

(**Opposite, above**) Marines from Companies B and D of the 1st Raider Battalion along with the 2nd Battalion, 5th Marines are shown landing from their LCVPs between 0800 and 0915 hours on Tulagi's southern coast on 7 August 1942. Lieutenant Colonel Merritt Edson's Raiders swept eastwards, while the elements of the 5th Marines moved westwards. It would not be until D+2 that Tulagi would be secured after fanatical Japanese SNLF resistance. *(NARA)*

(**Opposite, below**) A Marine ground crew is shown putting out a fire on a USMC F4 Wildcat fighter. The Marines' 'Cactus Air Force' at Henderson Field was constantly targeted by Japanese aerial and naval bombardment. In order for the Marines to hold Guadalcanal after the amphibious landing of 7 August 1942 by the 1st Marine Division (Reinforced), the airfield had to be defended as an 'unsinkable aircraft carrier' with its aircraft remaining serviceable. The Japanese expended increasing air, naval and ground forces to capture Henderson Field, which detracted supplies and reinforcements from their Papua New Guinea campaign. *(NARA)*

(**Opposite, above**) Three 11th Marines are shown sighting their 75mm pack howitzer which, along with 105mm howitzers, provided devastating fire to break up enemy ground attacks against the Henderson Field perimeter. The 75mm pack howitzer was small and easy to move ashore, as well as break down into component parts for movement to other positions. *(NARA)*

(**Opposite, below**) A Marine is seen here inspecting the wreckage of an IJA Type 97 *Chi-Ha* medium tank that was destroyed at the mouth of the Matanikau River on 23 October 1942. Japanese leadership was committed to re-taking Guadalcanal and compelling Major General Alexander A. Vandergrift to surrender his 1st Marine Division (Reinforced), along with elements of the US Army's Americal Division that joined the island combat. As Japanese reinforcements of troops, armour, planes and ships were added to the Guadalcanal cauldron, Japanese outpost operations along Papua New Guinea's northern coast at Buna, Gona and Sanananda received minimal additional support. *(NARA)*

(**Above**) Soldiers of the 35th IR, 25th Division are shown loading ammunition for their .30 calibre machine guns, which was parachuted down in an ammunition sack onto their ridgeline by USAAF aircraft on Guadalcanal in late January 1943. Due to the remoteness of their positions to expel the Japanese from Guadalcanal, this was the most expeditious method of getting critical supplies to the soldiers. *(NARA)*

An Australian soldier is shown casually regarding a monument to the officers and men who died defending Turnbull Field, the westernmost part of the Japanese advance at Milne Bay in late August–early September 1942. Eighty-five unknown Japanese SNLF troops were interred there. At Milne Bay, it was the fighting élan of Australian soldiers that first broke the spell of Japanese invincibility. *(NARA)*

(**Opposite, above**) Due to a paucity of Allied shipping, two Australians are shown having commandeered an intact, captured Japanese landing barge or *Daihatsu* in Papua's eastern coastal waters after the battle at Milne Bay was won in early September 1942. Two smaller sailing craft, which were also employed to ferry supplies, are seen in the background. *(NARA)*

(**Opposite, below**) Australian gunners of the 1st Mountain Battery are shown unloading a 3.7in mountain howitzer from a commandeered Japanese landing barge in the coastal waters of northern Papua near Embogo in the late autumn of 1942. This two-gun section of 3.7in mountain artillery fired a 20-pound projectile with a maximum range of 6,000 yards. *(NARA)*

43
8
6

(**Opposite, above**) Australian soldiers from the 18th Brigade's 2/9th Infantry Battalion are shown advancing through the Duropa Plantation's thick undergrowth while following an Australian-crewed M3 Stuart light tank in December 1942. Tank-infantry cooperation proved to be an essential tactic with the Stuart's turret gun providing direct fire against Japanese pillboxes and bunkers, while the latter protected the M3 light tank from suicidal infantry rushes with demolitions and hand grenades. *(NARA)*

(**Above**) Three 127th IR soldiers on the Urbana Force front are shown in a captured, well-camouflaged Japanese trench near Buna Village in mid-December. The two standing soldiers have their M1 Garand semi-automatic rifles at the ready, while the third infantryman (right) is crawling through a communication trench. *(NARA)*

(**Opposite, below**) In early January after Buna fell, Australian 18th Brigade infantrymen are shown re-deploying through the US 128th IR lines to the Sanananda sector on the western side of the Girua River to relieve the remnants of the 126th IR that fought with the AIF 7th Division. Elements of the 1st and 3rd battalions, 126th IR and the depleted Australian 21st Brigade that manned roadblocks on the Soputa-Sanananda MT (Motor Transport) Road suffered heavy casualties. *(NARA)*

(**Above**) Soldiers of the US 127th IR are shown advancing westward from Buna in single file through a muddy area along the coastal track to move on Giruwa. On 5 January, Company G, 127th IR crossed the Siwori Creek and moved westward. During that movement, the Americans were engaged by elements of Colonel Yazawa's 1st Battalion, 170th IR (the Nojiri Battalion). The Japanese were tenacious and abandoned their positions only when they were about to be overrun. The soldiers of the 127th IR also deployed a 37mm AT gun that poured canister into the Japanese infantry in order to advance. *(NARA)*

(**Opposite, above**) A US Fifth Air Force B-25 twin-engined medium Mitchell bomber is shown in a low-level strafing run with multiple nose-mounted MGs and a 20mm cannon against a Japanese freighter off the northern coast of Papua in 1942. The splash shown to the right of the aircraft was a previous B-25's 'skip-bombing' of the Japanese vessel. Lieutenant General George Kenney's aircrews perfected a number of different aerial attack methods that interdicted both Japanese troop reinforcement and re-supply efforts for their garrisons at Buna, Gona and Sananananda along Papua's northern coast. *(NARA)*

(**Opposite, below**) A USN Lockheed PV-1 Ventura (also called a B-34 Lexington by the USAAF) twin-engine bomber takes off from the newly-completed airfield in the Russell Islands for a sortie against Japanese targets in the Central Solomons. Originally, the Lockheed Ventura was built to replace the older Lockheed Hudson bomber/patrol plane, the latter having fared poorly against the Japanese in the skies over Malaya. The plane had a crew of six and a range of over 1,600 miles with a service ceiling of 26,000ft. It mounted four .50in calibre and two .30in calibre Browning machine guns, in addition to carrying a 3,000lb bomb load, one torpedo or six depth-charges. In the South Pacific, the Royal New Zealand Air Force (RNZAF) flew these aircraft from fields in Fiji prior to missions from Henderson Field and the Russell Islands (as shown here), while the Australians flew them over New Guinea along with the more famous B-25 Mitchell bombers. *(NARA)*

Munda Airfield, seen with Blanche Channel (right), was the objective of Admiral Halsey's invasion of New Georgia and the surrounding islands. Scattered Japanese aircraft were in their revetments with bomb hits on nearby higher points such as Biblio and Kokengolo Hills, the latter from which the Japanese commander, Major General Minoru (Noboru) Sasaki, observed the Rendova landings on 30 June 1943. *(NARA)*

Marine Raiders crouch amid the dense jungle vegetation on the way from Rice Anchorage to Enogai Inlet in early July 1943. The Raiders had their march towards Enogai Inlet punctuated by attacks from IJA and SNLF infantry in company and larger strength. *(NARA)*

A Marine Raider detachment crosses a malaria-infested jungle swamp on the way from Rice Anchorage to Enogai Inlet, which was just 2 miles from Bairoko Harbour. In addition to enemy attacks, the swollen waterways and thick mud from the torrential rains posed obstacles to the movement of Colonel Harry Liversedge's troops. A Marine (third from left) is shouldering a Boys AT rifle, which could penetrate only lightly-armoured tanks. *(NARA)*

(**Above**) A Marine examines equipment left behind in a Japanese bomb shelter. This coconut-log-reinforced entrenchment would probably require a direct aerial bomb or a heavy-calibre artillery shell to reduce it had the Japanese not abandoned this position on the orders of General Sasaki in the waning days of the campaign to seize Munda Airfield during the first week of August 1943. Fortified positions such as these were now characteristic of Japanese island defence across the Pacific. *(NARA)*

(**Opposite, above**) An iconic photograph of American soldiers of the 172nd IR, 43rd Division at the water's edge after landing at Rendova Point during a rainstorm on 30 June 1943. The landing would place the Americans in close proximity to Munda Airfield across Blanche Channel on nearby New Georgia Island. *(NARA)*

(**Opposite, below**) USN LSTs with their bow ramps lowered at the shoreline are unloaded by soldiers on Rendova. Atop the vessels, wary sailors stand by their anti-aircraft guns to fire on the predictable low-flying enemy fighter sweeps. *(NARA)*

354

(**Above**) In early August 1943, a column of M3 light Stuart tanks from one of the Marine Defence Battalions on New Georgia advances along a heavily-wooded island trail to support Army infantry units advancing on Japanese defences to get to Munda Airfield. The Stuart tanks on New Georgia, like those on New Guinea, were also used as 'mobile pillboxes' to neutralize the extensive Japanese entrenchments that housed light artillery, MGs and riflemen. The main 37mm turret gun and MGs provided suppressive fire as well as armour-piercing rounds to penetrate the coral, logs and earth reinforcement to the enemy pillboxes. Despite the tanks' firepower, the relentless Japanese infantry still attacked the M3s with flame-throwers, grenades and magnetic mines, which disabled a few during the slow advance on Munda. *(NARA)*

(**Opposite, above**) A dead Japanese infantryman is shown after having committed suicide by discharging his *Arisaka* rifle with his bare toe into his head. The Japanese warrior code (*Bushido*) emphasized death rather than surrender. This ideology was demonstrated throughout the entire Pacific War. *(NARA)*

(**Opposite, below**) A Marine Vought F4U-1 Corsair takes off from battle-scarred Munda Airfield. The Corsair, with its inverted gull-wing design, was planned as a carrier-borne fighter for the USN. However, as both carrier-related problems and ground combat success would soon demonstrate, it became an excellent ground-attack and close-support fighter, which fulfilled Marine aviation philosophy to lend assistance to the Corps' rifle platoons on the ground reach their objective with a minimum of casualties. The Corsair entered operational service in 1943. The aircraft was armed with external bombs or a rocket load of 2,000lb to complement the six 0.50in-calibre forward-firing machine guns in the leading edges of the wings. This Marine aircraft would play a pivotal role in reducing Japanese dug-in positions on Peleliu. *(NARA)*

An Australian 40mm Bofors AA gun is seen in action against Japanese aircraft at Lae after its capture in September 1943 by the AIF 9th Division. MacArthur utilized multiple axes of advance to deplete Lae's garrison before its capture. After the bloody battles for Buna, Gona and Sananada in Papua, MacArthur had limited numbers of American infantrymen and relied on Australian infantry to fight into Northeast New Guinea's Markham River Valley and Huon Peninsula. *(NARA)*

An Australian 25th Brigade infantryman with his shouldered 'Owen Gun' and an American paratrooper are shown greeting one another in the Markham River Valley in September 1943. On 5 September, the US 503rd PIR captured the airfield at Nadzab, 20 miles north-west of Lae in a *coup de main* low-level parachute assault. With the airfield seized by the Americans, the Australian 7th Division's 25th Brigade was airlifted in compelling the Japanese to abandon Salamaua well to the south-east. *(NARA)*

Australian Chaplain Captain Jenson Scherwin of the AIF's 5th Division in I Corps is shown raising his country's flag in Salamaua on 11 September 1943 after securing the airfield there. Chaplain Scherwin had previously fled from his parish there with the Japanese landings in the early spring of 1942. (*NARA*)

(**Above**) An Australian infantryman of the AIF 9th Division's 28th Brigade is shown carrying one of his wounded comrades near the village of Sattelberg in November 1943. A Matilda Infantry tank of C Squadron, 1st Tank Battalion is seen in the background as these more heavily-armoured tracked vehicles replaced the lighter M3 Stuarts. MacArthur delivered the Australian 20th Brigade with his 7th Amphibious Fleet to attack Sattelberg on the Australian trek to capture Finschhafen. The Australians found thousands of Japanese at Finschhafen and it took reinforcements and two months to secure that area on the Huon Peninsula. *(NARA)*

(**Opposite, above**) New Zealand troops, after having unloaded supplies from their assault boats, move into the interior of one of the Treasury Islands south of Bougainville on 27 October 1943 in order to distract the Japanese commanders' attention away from the main amphibious operation on Cape Torokina in Empress Augusta Bay on 1 November. Also, as a diversion on the night of 28 October, the 2nd Marine Parachute Battalion was inserted onto Choiseul, a large Northern Solomon Island to Bougainville's south-east. With Allied threats to the south and south-east of Bougainville prior to Halsey's invasion at Empress Augusta Bay, the Japanese re-allocated their defences against these diversions accordingly and neglected reinforcing Bougainville's western coast at Cape Torokina. *(NARA)*

(**Opposite, below**) As with previous operations in the Southern and Central Solomon Islands, the movements of supplies from the beachhead inland to avoid exposure to enemy air attacks continued at Bougainville. Here, Marine work details labour after securing the Torokina landing beaches, unload supplies and ammunitions from LCVPs. A 0.75-ton utility truck, which has just been loaded with munitions, begins to move across the beachhead through some deep sand to the front lines. *(NARA)*

17
KS

Marines are shown atop an M3 half-track serving as a 75mm GMC delivered by an LCVP in a subsequent landing wave at Torokina. This was the primary American heavy TD in combat during 1942–43. It suffered from a very limited traverse and an inadequate cross-country speed. However, neither of these detriments interfered with its combat use on the South Pacific Islands. *(NARA)*

Soldiers of the 145th IR, 37th Division are shown manning their 0.30-calibre, water-cooled Browning 1917 MG in a reinforced bunker in the Torokina perimeter as they await the massive Japanese counterattack in early March 1944. IJA 17th Army commander, Lieutenant General Harukichi Hyakutake, amassed more than 15,000 infantry and artillery troops; the latter manning 75mm pack howitzers and 105mm and 150mm guns, which were hauled onto ridges dominating the perimeter. This was the greatest concentration of IJA forces that would fight in the South Pacific. It was not larger because the remaining 18,000 troops of the 17th Army were needed to hold the rest of Bougainville's northern and southern ends at Buka and Buin respectively. *(NARA)*

The fighter strip at Cape Torokina's shoreline as seen in late 1944 from an aircraft flying over it. Eight USN Seabee battalions and one New Zealand engineer brigade began work on a fighter strip at the edge of Cape Torokina at a relatively dry area in Empress Augusta Bay on 10 November 1943. Remarkably, the fighter strip was ready for operation on 10 December, when Marine F4U Corsairs flew into their new base. *(NARA)*

Marines are seen here using the protection of the Burns Phillips Pier to get ashore at Red Beach on 20 November 1943 on Tarawa Atoll's Betio Island in the Gilbert Islands. Due to a low tide, even shallow-draft Higgins boats transporting the 2nd Marine Division's assault wave were unable to clear the reef, leaving riflemen as far as 500 yards from shore. As amphibious tracked vehicles were utilized to clear the reef to get onto the assault beaches, they were set ablaze by Japanese gunfire from fortified bunkers near the water's edge. *(NARA)*

(**Opposite, above**) Two infantrymen are shown here with their flame-thrower at a Japanese pillbox as the American soldiers mounted an attack from their perimeter to eliminate enemy infiltration on 17 March 1944 on Bougainville. The soldiers were from the 2nd Battalion of an HQ company of the 37th Infantry Division. *(NARA)*

(**Opposite, below**) The 2nd Division Marines take cover from enemy fire while manning a 0.30in-calibre LMG behind a Betio Island demolished seawall in Tarawa Atoll. The Marines and some attached US Army 27th Division infantrymen assaulted the Gilbert Islands from 20 to 23 November 1943, paying a steep price in bloodshed (3,200 Marine casualties) against fanatic Japanese 7th Sasebo SNLF and 3rd Special Base Defence Force troops. This initial US offensive in the CPA ominously presaged suicidal enemy defences at the landing beaches. Only one Japanese officer and sixteen enlisted men surrendered from a garrison of more than 3,500 at Tarawa. *(NARA)*

(**Above**) The 2nd Division Marines are shown attacking a Japanese fortified mound of sand, earth and coral (background). Many of these 'pillboxes' were strengthened with coconut logs to withstand naval and aerial bombardment. American light and medium tanks along with Marine flame-thrower and demolition teams were required to reduce the Japanese bunkers in addition to a Marine riflemen rush. *(NARA)*

(**Opposite, above**) Two 7th Sasebo SNLF soldiers are shown lying dead in their pillbox after committing ritual suicide according to the *Bushido* code rather than surrender. Note the nature of the extensive coconut log fortification to this bunker. A gas mask is lying on the pillbox floor (right foreground). The tenacity of the Japanese defenders and the bombproof construction of enemy emplacements on Betio Island in the Tarawa Atoll contributed to the very heavy 2nd Marine Division's death and casualty tolls in capturing this Gilbert Island locale. *(NARA)*

(**Opposite, below**) US Army troops from the 112th Cavalry Regiment are shown disembarking from their LCVP at Arawe on New Britain's southern tip on 15 December 1943 to serve as a diversion to the upcoming amphibious assault at Cape Gloucester. A Marine Amphibian Tractor Battalion company with their LVTs also took part in the landings. The two-company-strong IJA garrison at Arawe dispersed and 1,000 IJA combat-seasoned troops left Cape Gloucester towards Arawe only days before the 1st Marine Division's amphibious assault at the former locale. *(NARA)*

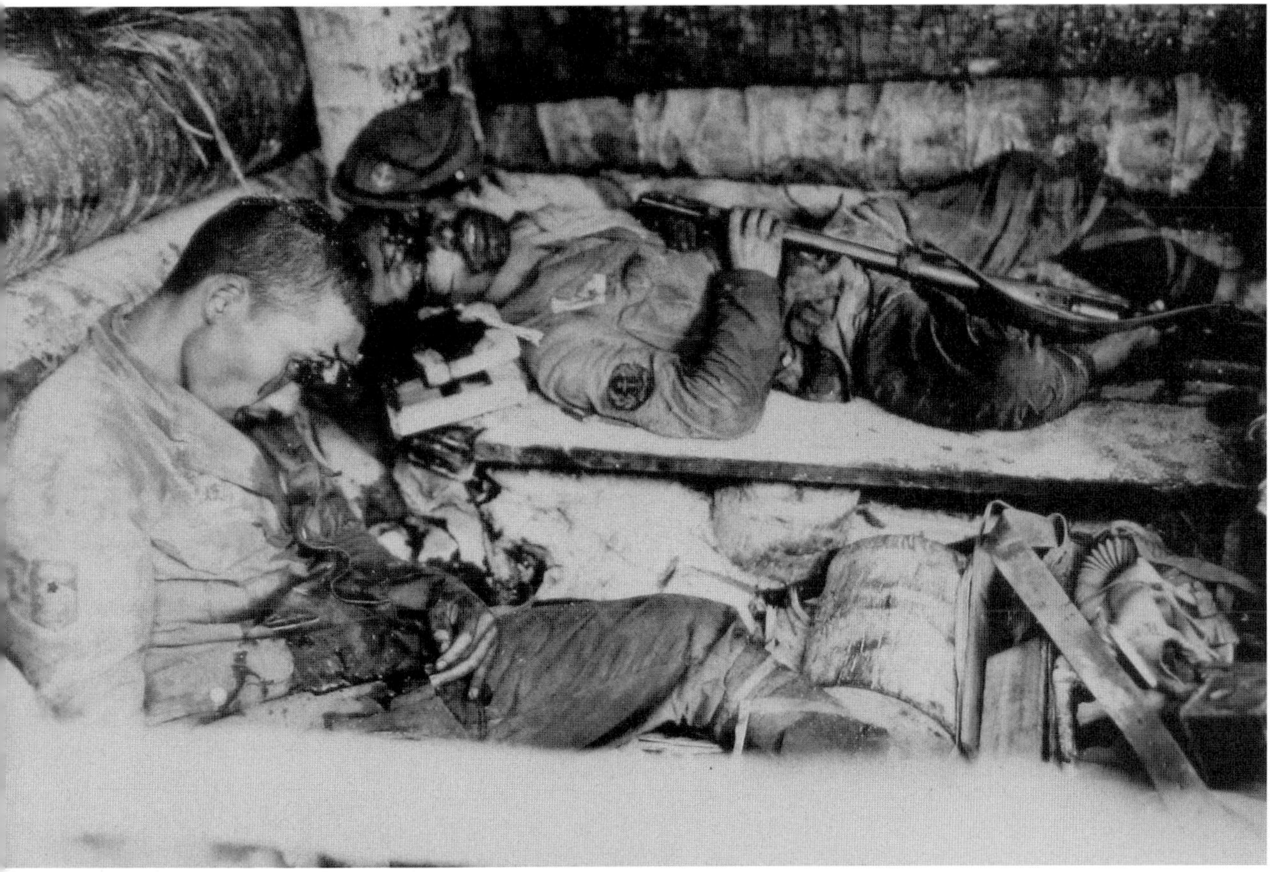

An assault wave of the 1st Marine Division, entirely under MacArthur's SWPA command and recuperated from its Guadalcanal ordeal, is shown advancing from their landing craft through the surf onto the shoreline of Cape Gloucester on New Britain's north-western tip on 26 December. The objective of the Marine landing was to deny the Japanese an opportunity to launch air strikes from nearby airfields against AIF troops advancing along Northwest New Guinea's coast on the Huon Peninsula between Finschhafen and Saidor *(NARA)*.

The 1st Division Marines are shown advancing past a destroyed Japanese aircraft at one of the twin airstrips captured after landing at Cape Gloucester and moving through the jungle in December 1943. USN Seabees attempted to repair the airfields from the pre-invasion bombardment; however, one was not located on suitable ground. Although one airfield briefly housed two US Fifth Air Force fighter squadrons, it was eventually abandoned as newer airfields were captured or constructed as the SWPA victories moved forward. *(NARA)*

A weary-looking 1st Division Marine is seen shouldering the barrel of his 0.30in-calibre Browning M1917 water-cooled MMG during the offensive through the jungles of western New Britain after the successful brief conquest of airfields in the Cape Gloucester area as the Japanese were withdrawing eastwards towards Rabaul on the northern tip of New Britain. A combat team of the 5th Marines landed along the western coast of the Willaumez Peninsula, to the east of Cape Gloucester along New Britain's northern coast on 6 March 1944 and advanced eastward through jungle and dense scrub towards a landing strip at Talasea on the peninsula's opposite coast, which they captured. Retreating Japanese defenders prevented the Marines from cutting off the withdrawing enemy falling back towards Rabaul from Cape Gloucester. More than 300 1st Division Marines died on New Britain and another 1,000+ were wounded in action. Nimitz withdrew the Marines from the Willaumez Peninsula in late March-early April and the entire 1st Marine Division went to a new training base on Pavuvu in the Russell Islands of the southern Solomon chain to receive extensive reinforcements, re-fit and prepare for the Peleliu invasion. *(NARA)*

W-CPA-44-106-N

(**Opposite, above**) Soldiers of the US 7th Infantry Division are shown approaching Kwajalein Island at the southern end of the Japanese-mandated Marshall Islands' Kwajalein Atoll. H-hour for the Kwajalein Island amphibious assault was 0930 hours on 1 February 1944. The 4th Marine Division amphibiously assaulted two other connected islands, Roi-Namur, at the northern end of Kwajalein Atoll. The Marshall Islands' capture yielded extant airfields to the USN and represented American penetration of Japan's 'outer ring' of defences in the CPA. *(NARA)*

(**Opposite, below**) A US Army 7th Infantry Division's 37mm AT gun is shown firing on Japanese positions on Kwajalein Island at the southern end of Kwajalein Atoll in the Marshall Islands. After landing at the island's southern end, the 7th Infantry Division's 184th and 32nd RCTs had to eliminate a number of Japanese inland fortifications and strongpoints as well as Japanese counterattacks. Major General Corlett, the 7th Division's commander, declared the Kwajalein Island secure at 1600 hours on 4 February. *(NARA)*

(**Above**) A Marine M4 medium tank called 'Jungle Jim' is shown landing on the twin Roi-Namur Islands in Kwajalein Atoll on 1 February 1944. Attached to the M4 unit was the 4th Light TB with M5 light tanks. Seizing Japanese airfields on Roi was the primary objective as well as subjugating Namur, which was connected to Roi via a sandbar. *(NARA)*

(**Above**) American landing craft are shown approaching a smoke-covered beachhead on Engebi Island in Eniwetok Atoll on 18 February 1944. Heavy naval pre-assault bombardment had detonated the main Japanese ammunition dump on the island. The 22nd Marines made the amphibious assault along Engebi's southern coast with the island's airfield to the west occupying the entire width of the island. *(NARA)*

(**Opposite, above**) One of only a few Japanese 37mm-gunned Type 95 *Ha-Go* light tanks is destroyed in the hull-down, dug-in position within a bomb crater on Engebi Island. The Marines M4A2 medium tanks with a 75mm turret gun easily knocked out Japanese lightly-armoured tanks, the latter to support elements of the IJN 1st and 61st Amphibious Brigades' defenders. Engebi Island was secured by the 22nd Marines at 1500 hours on 18 February 1944. *(NARA)*

(**Opposite, below**) A 22nd Marines rifleman inspects the corpse of a dead Japanese soldier near a 'spider hole' at the base of a blasted tree trunk on Parry Island in Eniwetok Atoll. All three 22nd Marines' battalions participated in the amphibious assault on and capture of heavily-defended Parry Island on 22 February. *(NARA)*

A wounded Marine from the 3rd Battalion, 22nd Marines is shown receiving first-aid by a Navy corpsman and a fellow rifleman on Eniwetok Island in Eniwetok Atoll. The 3rd Battalion, 22nd Marines, using shallow-draft and armoured tracked vessels, landed on Eniwetok Island on 19 February with the 1st and 3rd Battalions, 106th IR of the Army's 27th Division. The Japanese learned that their shoreline fortifications were too vulnerable to USN and aerial bombardment, so they retreated to successive defensive lines along the length of Eniwetok Island, which was secured by 21 February. *(NARA)*

The 126th RCT from the 32nd Division disembarks from their LCVPs at Saidor on the north-west coast of the Huon Peninsula on 2 January 1944. These American soldiers were trying to trap 12,000 Japanese troops that had been defeated on the peninsula by the Australians, who were still pursuing them. This landing advanced MacArthur's forces about 100 miles further westward along the northern New Guinea coast. *(NARA)*

Lieutenant General Walter Krueger, commander of US Sixth Army, is shown here walking along the beach at Hollandia in April 1944. Accompanying him is Major General Horace Fuller, commander of the US 41st Infantry Division, which had been in combat since Buna and Sananada Point in Papua in January 1943. *(NARA)*

(**Opposite, above**) A RAN-crewed LCVP is shown landing American infantrymen atop jeeps at Hollandia in April 1944. To the right, a larger LST, which was able to come up near the shoreline, was able to unload infantry, tanks, half-tracks and other vehicles and had an array of AA deck guns to thwart any Japanese air-raid. *(NARA)*

(**Opposite, below**) A mortar crew of the 41st Division marches inland from the Hollandia beachhead with its weapon broken down for the trek. Others carry mortar rounds in tubes as well as their M1 carbines as personal weapons against any Japanese that are hiding in the jungle along the way. *(NARA)*

(**Above**) Soldiers of the 163rd RCT, 41st Division as well as the 127th RCT, 32nd Division, both having been refitted in Australia by General Eichelberger, land on Aitape Beach on 22 April 1944. The three closest soldiers are all armed with the M1 carbine, which was a compact weapon for operations in the jungle. However, many riflemen claimed that the gun lacked stopping power, although it fired a 0.30in-calibre bullet. It was a semi-automatic like the M1 Garand rifle and weighed about 4lb less, even though it has a fifteen- or thirty-round detachable box magazine. *(NARA)*

4

(**Opposite, above**) A USN carrier-based Grumman TBF Avenger soars over Tanahmerah Bay as landing craft race for the assault beach on 22 April 1944. Troops met with little opposition and advanced quickly, although moving supplies from the beach became a logistical nightmare. The TBF Avenger, after its disastrous debut at the Battle of Midway in June 1942, developed into one of the classic torpedo-bombers of the war. *(NARA)*

(**Above**) An LCM unloads American soldiers and a pillbox-smashing tank at the beachhead at Tanahmerah Bay on 22 April 1944. The beach sand at Tanahmerah Bay was very dense, which impeded a rapid advance of the 24th Division. Congestion and supply problems at Tanahmerah Bay ensued since it was impossible to get vehicles off the beach. The 24th Division soldiers had to hand-carry all their supplies and for weeks lived on half-rations. *(NARA)*

(**Opposite, below**) The first wave of the 1st Cavalry Division (G Troop, 2nd Squadron, 5th Cavalry Regiment) in their older Eureka assault craft are shown landing on Los Negros in the Admiralty Islands on 2 May 1944. The amphibious operation's aims were to secure Seeadler Harbour, an excellent anchorage on the north coast, and Momote airfield on the southern coast. *(NARA)*

(**Opposite, above**) The first wave of elements of the 163rd RCT, 41st Division hits the beach at Wakde Island on 18 May 1944. The previous day, elements of this formation landed unopposed in Maffin Bay near Sarmi. Wakde Island proved to be a much more difficult mission. It took two days of close fighting to wrest the roughly 800 Japanese troops from their 'spider holes', coconut log bunkers and caves. *(USAMHI)*

(**Opposite, below**) Riflemen from the 2nd Marine Division are shown crawling along a contested beachhead at Saipan. An LVT(A) is shown in the background (right). Variants of these LVT(A) craft had different turret armament ranging from an M3 light tank turret with a 37mm gun to a 75mm howitzer mounted in the turret of the M8 HMC as the former gun calibre proved to be too light to demolish enemy fortifications at the shoreline. *(NARA)*

(**Above**) Two Marines on Saipan are shown here tossing percussion grenades into a Japanese pillbox. The Marine to the right is shown standing alert with his M1 Garand semi-automatic rifle for any enemy soldiers that might have emerged after the grenades exploded. Saipan, in the Mariana Islands, was invaded on 15 June 1944 and was not secured until 9 July with the US 2nd Marine and the US 27th Infantry Divisions having successfully defeated the IJA 43rd Division, commanded by Lieutenant General Yoshitsugu Saito. Successful American invasions of Guam and Tinian in the Marianas followed. The Marianas seizures shortened the range for American B-29 bombers to 1,300 miles from Japan's Home Islands. The Superfortresses also regularly attacked Japanese installations in the Philippines for MacArthur's upcoming invasion. Japanese air attacks, principally launched from Iwo Jima, against the newly-operational American Superfortress aerodromes were a predictable enemy response to the Marianas' conquest. *(NARA)*

(**Opposite, above**) A trio of 2nd Division Marines is seen gazing through the ruined buildings of Garapan, the largest town on Saipan, in July 1944. In addition to loss of almost 30,000 IJA soldiers, close to 1,000 Japanese civilians on Saipan committed suicide during the last days of the battle. Many jumped from seaside heights that were later designated 'Suicide' and 'Banzai' cliffs, in addition to dying during combat in locales such as Garapan. *(NARA)*

(**Above**) A squad of Marines is seen here warily approaching Garapan on Saipan in July 1944 along a road flanked by elevated terrain beside it. The Marines sought protection from enemy fire from the ridge behind an M4 medium tank named 'King Kong'. The M4 medium tank was versatile with a 75mm turret gun and assorted MGs to combat Japanese emplacements holding up Marine riflemen advances. *(NARA)*

(**Opposite, below**) On 21 July 1944, soldiers of the 77th Division's 305th IR are shown disembarking from their LVTs onto a Guam assault beach to re-capture the former American possession, which was the largest and most southernmost of the Marianas, approximately 28 miles long and 4 to 8 miles wide. The 305th IR assisted the Marines' 1st Provisional Brigade to capture Mount Alifan the next day and also took the summit of Mount Tenjo on 28 July after repelling a strong Japanese counterattack along the Orote Peninsula made by the IJA 10th Independent Mixed Brigade on 25–26 July. *(NARA)*

A Marine patrol carrying an M1917 0.30in-calibre water-cooled MMG is shown trudging along a path through some rough, hilly terrain on Guam in July 1944. The Marines' 1st Provisional Brigade comprised the 22nd Marines, veterans of Eniwetok Atoll in the Marshall Islands campaign, and the re-constituted 4th Marines. The 4th Marines was re-designated as such to honour the similarly-named Marine regiment that was lost in the Philippines in 1942. *(NARA)*

(**Opposite, above**) Soldiers of the 77th Division's 306th IR are shown mopping up last-ditch Japanese positions on Guam during early autumn 1944. This regiment landed at Agat Bay on 23 July and encountered strong Japanese resistance on the island. Following a massive air bombardment on 7 August, the entire 77th Division launched an attack with the Marine formations to clear the northern third of Guam. *(NARA)*

(**Opposite, below**) At Pacific Fleet HQ in Pearl Harbor, Admiral Nimitz, C-in-C Pacific Fleet, is shown pointing at a map of the Far East. He is joined (from left to right) by General Douglas A. MacArthur, C-in-C SWPA, President Franklin D. Roosevelt and JCOS member Admiral William Leahy. At this conference on Oahu on 26 July 1944, Nimitz proposed an invasion of Japanese-controlled Formosa and, perhaps, seizing East China coast bases as a prelude to a Central Pacific Area (CPA) advance on the Ryuku Islands and then Japan's Home Islands. With this CPA offensive, the Philippines would be bypassed. MacArthur countered that this would be a grave error for Roosevelt to make as the SWPA commander had promised to the Filipino people an American liberation of their islands as soon as feasible. MacArthur won the debate with an agreement to invade the southern Philippine island of Mindanao in the autumn of 1944. Peleliu and Angaur were to be assaulted in the Palau Island group in September 1944 to 'cover MacArthur's right flank'. *(NARA)*

American soldiers of the 41st Division's 163rd RCT ford the shallow mouth of the Driniumor River in August 1944 to sever the advance of several thousand Japanese being rushed from the bypassed stronghold, Wewak in the east, to interfere with MacArthur's other westward amphibious advances. Another American unit, Ted Force, comprising the 124th RCT of the 31st Infantry Division at Aitape, also moved onto the Driniumor River to set up a defensive perimeter against the westward-advancing Japanese infantry from Wewak. Japanese 18th Army commander, General Adachi, planned to breach the Driniumor River line at a point 3,000 yards inland to envelop the Americans' right flank there with his IJA 20th and 41st divisions. *(NARA)*

American soldiers are shown here covering an entrance to a hut while searching for Japanese soldiers in hiding on Morotai Island in the Halmahera group of the eastern NEI's Molucca chain. The invasion force of the 155th IR, 31st Division landed on Morotai Island on 15 September 1944 without any Japanese opposition. The operation's intent was to cover MacArthur's 'left flank' from a Japanese attack for his proposed assault on the southern Philippine island of Mindanao. *(NARA)*

Chapter Two

Terrain, Fortifications and Weapons

Terrain

The Palau Islands are the westernmost of the Caroline Islands, a 2,000-mile east-to-west chain north of the equator and were named by Spanish explorers in the late seventeenth century for their King Charles II. The major islands in the Western Carolines are Ulithi, Yap and the Palau group. The Palau Group (see Map 5) extends for around 110 miles and contains more than a hundred islands and islets. Babelthuap, to the north, is the largest island, being 10 miles by 16 miles, and is 795ft above sea level. More importantly, the Japanese built an airfield at its south-east end.

To the immediate south of Babelthuap is the small island of Koror. This is where the Japanese had their administrative centre, a naval HQ, a seaplane base and AA defences. Near to Koror was Arakabesan Island, which housed seaplane and submarine bases. Most of the indigenous inhabitants were on Babelthuap and Koror.

There are numerous tiny limestone islets situated between Koror and Peleliu, 25 miles to the south-west. Peleliu is approximately 6 miles long and 2 miles wide in the south. Angaur is the southernmost of the Palau Islands, located 7 miles from Peleliu. The Palau Islands, with the exception of Angaur, are almost entirely situated within coral barrier reefs, which provide protection and lagoons for surface vessel anchorage.

Most of the Palau Islands are flat, rising from the sea with elevations of less than 100ft. However, on Peleliu (see Map 6), there is a well-defined elevated limestone outcropping, which is 550ft above sea level at its highest point and spans the island's entire peninsula from south-west to north-east as a collection of hills and steep ridges which overlook a large portion of the island including the Japanese-built two-runway airfield. In the centre of the peninsula, this mass of undulating hills, ridges and ravines, instead of a single connected highland, is referred to as Umurbrogol Mountain, with 500 natural and Japanese-excavated caves, the latter often with interconnecting tunnels, tiers and galleries.

An area of the Umurbrogol Mountain, the 'Umurbrogol Pocket', was about 400 by 1,200 yards and situated in the most rugged, worst part of the ridges. Access to the

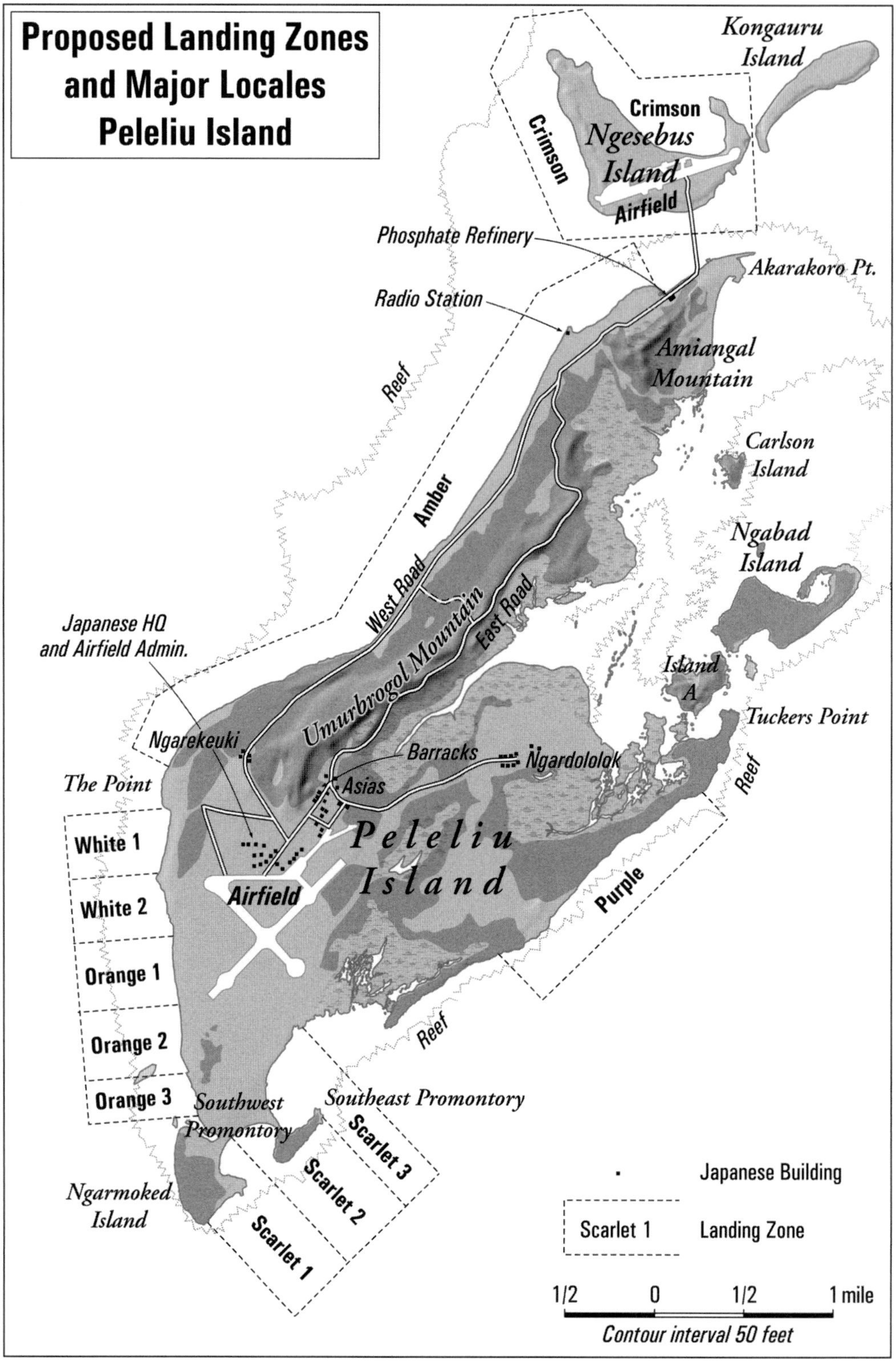
Proposed Landing Zones and Major Locales Peleliu Island
Kongauru Island
Crimson
Crimson
Ngesebus Island
Airfield
Phosphate Refinery
Akarakoro Pt.
Radio Station
Amiangal Mountain
Reef
Carlson Island
Amber
Ngabad Island
West Road
East Road
Umurbrogol Mountain
Japanese HQ and Airfield Admin.
Island A
Tuckers Point
Ngarekeuki
Barracks
Ngardololok
The Point
Asias
Reef
White 1
Peleliu Island
White 2
Airfield
Purple
Orange 1
Reef
Orange 2
Orange 3
Southwest Promontory
Southeast Promontory
Scarlet 3
Scarlet 2
Scarlet 1
Ngarmoked Island
Japanese Building
Scarlet 1
Landing Zone
1/2 0 1/2 1 mile
Contour interval 50 feet

ridge's peak can only be gained by scaling the smaller surrounding heights. This was a hellacious terrain feature, inundated with gorges and caves. Many of the ridges, which were once covered with dense forests, were now transformed into a mass of sponge-like rock crevices and crags as natural erosion and the Japanese removed the vegetation, creating terrain fortifications with interlocking fields of enemy fire from two or more positions.

Heavy rainfall (greater than 140in annually) and high temperatures (80–100° F) throughout other parts of Peleliu have enabled the growth of heavy vegetation composed of hardwood trees, palm species and dense, often impenetrable mangrove swamps, especially on the eastern side of the island. Humidity of over 80 per cent occurs during the hottest months of June to September and accompanies the heaviest rainfall. Extreme fatigue and thirst are the results of this climate, especially under arduous combat conditions.

Map 6. Proposed Landing Zones and Major Locales on Peleliu Island. Peleliu is an island surrounded by a coral reef, which necessitated the transfer of US Marines from LCVPs to amphibious tracked vehicles to cross the reef onto the shoreline. Numerous potential landings sites were evaluated; however, five beaches on the western side of Peleliu proximate to the airfield were selected and included White 1 and 2, plus Orange 1, 2 and 3. 'The Point', which did not appear on any Marine planning maps, was an elevated Japanese defensive position at the far left of the American assault beaches in the 1st Marines' sector. Ngarmoked Island was on the far right of the Marine landing zones. The south-east and south-west promontories were Japanese artillery positions on peninsulas emanating from Peleliu well to the south of the airfield.

The two-runway airfield was situated on Peleliu's flat terrain with the Japanese administration building and barracks in proximity to the airfield's immediate north-east. Between the villages of Asias and Ngarekeuki was the start of the Umurbrogol Mountain range, which is an elevated limestone outcrop, 550ft above sea level at its highest point and spanning the island's entire length from south-west to north-east. Not truly a 'mountain', Umurbrogol Mountain comprised a collection of hills and steep ridges overlooking a large portion of the island including the airfield and contained 500 caves with interconnecting tunnels. This elevated terrain started north-east of the airfield and was intersected by numerous small valleys and ravines. Within Umurbrogol Mountain was a 400 by 1,200-yard area of extremely rugged terrain called the 'Umurbrogol Pocket' that was assaulted from all directions by rotating Marine and Army units from 27 September to 27 November.

The high ground of Peleliu's north-western peninsula is divided into three areas. Southernmost and most formidable was Umurbrogol Mountain. Kamilianlul Mountain (see Map 7) is also a misnomer as it was a continuation of the same Umurbrogol Mountain but lower, narrower and less rugged. The broad saddle of Kamilianlul Mountain separated it from Amiangal Mountain, the north-west peninsula's northernmost formation.

Peleliu's north-west peninsula, on which the Umurbrogol Mountain range is situated, extends in a north-eastward direction past the Radio Station and phosphate refinery along the island's West Road to Akarakoro Point.

To the immediate north of Akarakoro Point are the islands of Ngesebus and Kongauru connected by a causeway. Construction of an airfield on Ngesebus Island was under way at the time of the American invasion. *(Meridian Mapping)*

Peleliu is shaped like a fish hook made from the north-eastward-running peninsula on the island's western side. The southern end of Peleliu has mostly low-elevation, scrub-covered areas. Along the south-western end of Peleliu, on relatively flat land, the Japanese built an X-shaped naval airfield, which was the Palaus' principal air installation with complete servicing facilities. The airfield comprised two intersecting strips and was crushed coral-surfaced. The bomber field was 1,000 yards long and the fighter strip was considerably shorter. The airfield's south-western end was in extreme proximity to Peleliu's western beaches.

West and East Roads were situated on either side of the Peleliu peninsula at the time of the invasion. To the north of Peleliu are Ngesebus and Kongauru Islands. A wooden causeway 600 yards long connected Ngesebus Island with Peleliu's northern peninsular tip near a phosphate refinery and Akarakoro Point, the latter in proximity to Amiangal Mountain, another collection of undulating ridges and ravines. A separate wooden causeway of 100 yards connected Kongauru and Ngesebus Islands to one another. The Japanese were constructing an auxiliary fighter airfield on Ngesebus Island.

As Peleliu's coconut tree-lined shoreline is entirely protected by coral reefs, there were only a few good landing beaches where the Americans could attempt amphibious assault. The northern beaches were not suitable for the Marines' assault since the area was not deep enough to secure a good lodgement. To the south-east, Peleliu's shoreline is lined with mangrove swamps with a fringing reef. At the very southern end of Peleliu are two very small peninsulas comprising Ngarmoked Island (3,500 yards long by 1,000 yards wide) and another narrow one. The landing areas adjacent to Ngarmoked Island contained bluffs, the south-western and south-eastern promontories respectively, which enfiladed the western beaches. This area was also situated near an inlet with swift tides nullifying an invasion there.

The airfield, which was the primary objective of the Marine D-Day assault, was located on Peleliu's only piece of flat land in the south-western part of the island, and the best amphibious access to it was via three west coast landing beach areas (see Chapter 4 for details). Here, the fringing reef required assault troops to move from flat-bottomed LCVPs emanating from transports to amphibious tracked vehicles to cross the coral; thus it was referred to as the 'transfer line'. According to American pre-invasion maps, the beaches were considered to be relatively flat and smooth; however, at the very northern end of the western invasion beaches was an elevated terrain feature, unknown to Marine planners, called 'The Point' and the 1st Marines were to incur many casualties there. Densely wooded areas started just a few yards from the shoreline. The Japanese believed that if the Americans were to attack Peleliu, they would land along the western beaches and therefore they planned their defences accordingly.

Near Peleliu's airfield, the Japanese built hangars, barracks, administrative buildings, radio and radio detection-finder stations. At the northern end of the north-east-running peninsula, the Japanese had built a phosphate refinery as well as a narrow-gauge railway to move the phosphate. The IJN's 214th Naval Construction Battalion began constructing underground caves a year before IJA troops arrived. Because of this temporal disparity, IJN caves were more elaborate and complex than IJA caves, which were usually more simple using natural cave features and structure. They were to serve as bombproof shelters, supply areas and underground troop quarters. As the US Marine and Army assaults continued their drives to conquer Peleliu, the caves were transformed into a last-ditch defensive line.

Angaur Island (see Map 9) is 7 miles to the south-west of Peleliu and is the southernmost of the Palau group. Angaur, at its northern and north-eastern ends, is not enclosed within the reef system. The island is 2.5 by 1.5 miles in size with rugged coral and limestone ridges. It had a phosphate plant and a narrow-gauge railway line to move its primary mined product. Most of Angaur possessed scrub brush and heavy woods. The Navy planners wanted Angaur seized since it was a strategic location from which the enemy could attack Marine positions on Peleliu and also because they wanted to construct a bomber airfield on Angaur's flat lands. Ultimately the new airfield there became unnecessary as other operations unfolded elsewhere.

Fortifications

Despite the absence of an all-out Japanese beachhead defence, the American landings on Peleliu were nonetheless hotly contested. D-Day for the 1st Marine Division was to be one of the bloodiest amphibious assaults of the Pacific War. Rather, the Japanese commanders on Peleliu placed its greatest emphasis on interior defences. The Emperor's military leaders ordered Peleliu to be suicidally defended from fortifications and strongpoints that emanated from the many natural and man-made caves housing artillery and heavy weapons on Umurbrogol Mountain overlooking the airfield and Marine landing beaches. Both types of caves had many feet of earth and limestone to protect the troops from the preparatory American naval and aerial bombardment, while elaborate camouflage hid them from US artillery-spotters, advancing infantry and armour. Some caves possessed tunnels with sharp turns which shielded dug-in Japanese troops inside from American flame-throwers. Most Japanese caves were stocked with ammunition, food and water for a tenacious, protracted defence.

The Japanese defenders employed both offshore obstacles and mines at the water's edge, which destroyed numerous Marine amphibious tractors and DUKWs. Routes moving inland from Peleliu's beaches were also heavily protected with more land mines, AT barriers and ditches, barbed wire and increasingly strong defensive positions. The AT traps and ditches inland from the beaches were crude and not much of a hindrance for American tracked vehicles to move forward. The enemy also built pillboxes and casemates with steel-reinforced concrete and coral prior to adding camouflage for concealed anti-boat artillery to cover the American landing sites with devastating fire.

Weapons

As there had been much ordnance lost in the defence of the Marianas, the IJA defenders on Peleliu were below strength and fielded only one battalion of 75mm artillery and one mortar company comprising ten 81mm pieces. The IJN garrison had several larger-calibre guns. The 42nd Independent AAA high-velocity guns could also be dually utilized for flat trajectory fire, which was to prove lethal for Marine landing craft on the D-Day assault beaches.

American amphibious forces had steadily improved in Pacific operations since the Guadalcanal invasion in August 1942. The costly landings at Betio Island in Tarawa Atoll in the Gilbert Islands campaign of November 1943 reinforced the need for amphibious tracked vehicles to be able to cross coral reef. Additional progress and learning continued with the Mariana Islands invasions from June to August 1944 with a variety of newer ships and assault craft, LVT(A)s, to not only have assault troops cross coral reefs but to possess added firepower to knock out enemy strongpoints until Marine M4 medium tanks could land. Other assault/transport vessels were designed to expeditiously offload supplies to support the landing waves moving inland. USN carrier aircraft and surface bombardment had intensified with devastating effects on both long- and short-range Japanese targets. Although naval gunfire from a variety of battleships, heavy cruisers and destroyers could obliterate fixed enemy fortifications with their flat trajectory guns, the Japanese had learned to take shelter within their coral and limestone caves and ridges, thereby withstanding even the heaviest of American naval or aerial bombardment.

(**Opposite, above**) The south and western ends of Peleliu seen from an American scout plane after the invasion. Inland from the western invasion beaches (foreground), where some USN vessels are seen, is the X-shaped airfield that once accommodated IJA and IJN bombers and fighters. Also an inlet with the south-east promontory is visible (background, right). *(NARA)*

(**Opposite, below**) Marines are seen here moving along flat terrain towards the airfield centre on D-Day+1. As one of the only dry flatlands on Peleliu, the Japanese built the airfield at this site. *(NARA)*

(**Above**) A pair of Marines is shown moving warily behind a destroyed enemy truck while approaching a high ridge to the airfield's north-east between Ngarekeuki and Asias that the Japanese called *Kansokuyama* at the southern end of Umurbrogol Mountain. The Marines referred to it as 'Hill 300', while soldiers of the 81st Division called it 'Old Baldy'. This height had a Japanese OP at its crest and was packed with interior cave systems. *(NARA)*

(**Opposite, above**) A Marine column is shown advancing onto a series of northern ridges referred to as the 'Umurbrogol Pocket'. Hellacious combat occurred with Marine and Army attacks on the cluster of ridges from all directions by rotating units from late September to late November when the 'Pocket' finally fell. *(NARA)*

(**Opposite, below**) The 81st Division tank-infantry action during a later stage of the island's combat is shown within 'Horseshoe Valley', dominated by surrounding ridges called 'Five Brothers' (left), the western face of Walt Ridge ('Hill 100', right) and 'Hill 140' (background, centre). The only source of fresh water for the Japanese in 'Horseshoe Valley' was Grinlinton Pond. These ridges comprised the central part of Umurbrogol Mountain. By 22 October, repeated US attacks cleared Walt Ridge and 'Horseshoe Valley' and then encroached on the northern series of ridges comprising the 'Umurbrogol Pocket'. *(NARA)*

(**Opposite, above**) Marine riflemen are shown advancing along a path following an M4 medium tank with the southern face of Hill 300 ('Old Baldy') looming over the southern entrance of 'Horseshoe Valley'. To Hill 300's north was another series of Japanese-occupied ridges: 'Five Sisters', originally called 'Bloody Nose Ridge' by the initial Marine units that assaulted it. *(NARA)*

(**Opposite, below**) Riflemen of the 1st Marines are shown moving in the lee of the 'Horseshoe Valley' causeway across the swamp with the southern face of Walt Ridge visible in the background. The Marines are seen approaching two M4 medium tanks disabled by Japanese land mines. The nearby swamp hindered the Marines' approach. Once across the causeway, the Marines would be in proximity to the East Road, which paralleled the eastern side of Walt Ridge. *(NARA)*

(**Above**) A Marine in the foreground is shown observing an amphibious tractor fitted with a Mk 1 flame-thrower fire a jet of flame at the opening of a Japanese-occupied cave on one of Umurbrogol Mountain's ridges. Both Army and Marine units repeatedly assaulted the Japanese defences in this 'pocket' of caves, ravines, gorges and crevasses. *(NARA)*

(**Opposite, above**) A small Peleliu ridge is seen with three caves having been blasted out. The Japanese cleared the hillside of its vegetation to create mutually supporting defence positions against the Americans who would be advancing along difficult terrain without suitable cover. *(NARA)*

(**Above**) A Marine is shown standing with his Thompson 0.45in-calibre SMG at the mouth of a rocky crevice at the base of a ridge in the 'Umurbrogol Pocket'. Even after flame-throwers, satchel charges and bazookas were used, Marine and Army infantrymen would resort to tossing in hand grenades with the use of semi-automatic weapon gunfire to definitively secure a Japanese position. *(NARA)*

(**Opposite, below**) The opening to a larger Japanese cave within Umurbrogol Mountain is seen after it was reduced by attacking Americans between late September and late November. The debris of the enemy defenders is seen in the foreground. *(NARA)*

A unit of the 7th Marines is seen climbing up a steep incline at the southern face of Walt Ridge north-east of the airfield (background). The swamp (left), over which a causeway was contested, was at the southern entrance to 'Horseshoe Valley'. *(NARA)*

A Marine patrol is seen advancing through dense brush during their approach to 'Suicide Ridge'. This was one of many close-quarter engagements along the ridges of Umurbrogol Mountain during which Marines, due to the terrain, used rifle and hand grenades as well as 'Molotov cocktails' to destroy Japanese positions there. *(NARA)*

Marines are shown carrying one of their dead comrades through a defile of the 'Five Sisters', which was a series of five separate hills each over 200ft high and separated from one another by steep cliffs. 'Five Sisters' was the southernmost of a series of ridges that comprised the western side of Umurbrogol Mountain. Attacks on 'Five Sisters' by units of the 2nd Battalion, 1st Marines and 2nd Battalion, 7th Marines commenced on D+4. *(NARA)*

A group of 81st Infantry Division soldiers are shown taking cover behind one of their M4 medium tanks during an assault on Japanese positions in the vicinity of 'China Wall' and 'Death Valley' on the western side of Umurbrogol Mountain. American engineer bulldozers created an earthen ramp to give tanks access to these ridges where hellacious combat occurred against 300 surviving entrenched Japanese during the last week of November. *(NARA)*

Several 11th Marine artillerymen are shown hoisting a pre-assembled 75mm pack howitzer up a steep ridge with a pulley system connected to a truck at the base of Hill 140, which was captured by the 2nd Battalion, 5th Marines on 11 October. The 11th Marines were eager to get 75mm pack howitzers atop Hill 140 to rain direct fire onto the nearest of 'Five Brothers' but also part of 'Horseshoe Valley' and the draw between Walt and Boyd Ridges. Once atop the ridge, Marine gunners fired point-blank into Japanese caves honeycombed within other ridges along the northern part of Umurbrogol Mountain. Other 75mm pack howitzers were raised to the summit of Wattie Ridge in order to fire into 'Horseshoe Valley' and the western base of Walt Ridge. *(NARA)*

A Marine patrol is shown removing 75mm rounds from the disabled M4 medium tank after its tread was destroyed by a Japanese land mine. This occurred in the relatively flat terrain in the vicinity of the airfield. *(NARA)*

Near the landing beaches, a Marine detachment is shown using a coral outcrop for cover on the otherwise open terrain. In addition to Japanese artillery and mortars, entrenched enemy MGs took a heavy toll on the Marines landing on 15 September. *(NARA)*

Marines from the 3rd Battalion, 5th Marines are shown using a Japanese AT ditch as a CP 200 yards from the Orange Beach 2 assault area. A similar Japanese AT trap was used as a 7th Marines battalion HQ at Orange Beach 3 before it became General Rupertus' first CP after he landed on D+1. *(NARA)*

Soldiers from the 81st Division are seen watching combat from the top of a hummock. The infantryman second from the right is cradling an air-cooled, holed-jacket Browning M1919A6 0.30in-calibre LMG, which could fire 400–600 rounds per minute. During the war, it became clear that the BAR, while portable, could not have a high sustained rate of fire due to its fixed barrel and twenty-round magazine. The M1919A6 was an attempt to parallel the excellent portable German MG 34 and 42 weapons used at the squad level. Entering service in the autumn of 1943, the M1919A6 had a bipod like the BAR, and was heavy but portable at 32lb. *(NARA)*

Soldiers from the 81st Infantry Division are shown at Dead Man's Curve seeking cover from enemy snipers behind an armoured amphibious tractor on the West Road. Although deemed secure since the 5th Marines drove to the north along the West Road, on 3 October (D+18) Colonel Joseph F. Hankins, CO, Division HQ Battalion, was killed there by a sniper's bullet. Hankins became the highest-ranking 1st Marine Division officer lost during Peleliu's combat. *(NARA)*

A Japanese pillbox is shown from the front with its firing port at the bottom partially obscured by camouflage. This fortification was entirely constructed from coral near the beachhead and then covered with rocks and foliage. *(NARA)*

A Japanese fortification is seen from the rear with its firing port in the background. This gun position was constructed from coral and had a coconut-log roof to help withstand USN gunfire during the pre-invasion bombardment. *(NARA)*

A Marine patrol equipped with a flame-thrower is shown attacking a Japanese pillbox just inland from the beach on D-Day. This ground-level enemy fortification, common at the beachhead, was dug into the coral. *(NARA)*

A Japanese tank trap is shown inland from White Beach 2, which was constructed to hinder the Marines' armoured advance to the southern tip of the airfield after the landings on 15 September. It comprised a ditch with coconut logs traversing upright trees and the stumps of others. *(NARA)*

(**Above**) A Marine (right) is shown peering into a coconut log-reinforced Japanese searchlight position held together by steel cable wire. A goal of Japanese pre-invasion construction efforts was to absorb the USN gun and air bombardment and then harass the landing forces after the fire lifted. IJN fortifications were better constructed than the IJA ones, principally due to time and material favouring the former. *(NARA)*

(**Opposite, above**) A Marine is shown examining a larger Japanese artillery fortification constructed from raised earth and reinforced with rocks and coconut logs. The wooden beam demonstrated how this position was able to accommodate a large-calibre artillery piece that wreaked havoc on the landing beaches and Marine assault vehicles. *(NARA)*

(**Opposite, below**) The interior of a Japanese 75mm artillery casemate is shown here. The walls of this position were reinforced with stacked logs and wooden ammunition boxes. *(NARA)*

(**Opposite, above**) A Japanese bomb shelter is shown with its wooden braces along with rock and concrete reinforcement. The rear entrance of the bomb shelter is shown here. Japanese infantry and gunners were able to wait out the pre-invasion USN bombardment before returning to their guns and pillboxes. *(NARA)*

(**Above**) Marines are shown taking shade along a ruined building in the former Japanese administration complex at the recently-captured airfield. Temperatures on Peleliu were over 100° F by midday, combined with extremely high humidity. These climatic features amplified the initial lack of water for the assaulting Marine battalions. Two Marine artillery spotters with binoculars are shown atop the roof of the larger administration building (background) as the terrain at the airfield was flat. *(NARA)*

(**Opposite, below**) A destroyed Japanese barracks near the airfield is shown here. Early on 16 September, a Marine rifle company, with tank support and after heavy preparatory bombardment, seized this building after a sharp fire-fight. *(NARA)*

(**Above**) A Marine M4 medium tank is shown moving past a recently-captured Japanese blockhouse. Blockhouses held up Marine infantry advances on D-Day and D+1. These fortifications were difficult to reduce with their 5ft steel-reinforced concrete walls. All Marine infantry weapons' rounds and 75mm tank shells bounced off the walls. Marine demolition teams had to place their TNT satchels under smokescreens to obscure the blockhouses' apertures and then detonate the explosives to capture them. *(NARA)*

(**Opposite, above**) A captured Japanese blockhouse is shown serving as a 7th Marines' Heavy Weapons Company CP on D+1 with the Marine (left) operating an SCR 300 radio connected to a field telephone. The non-penetrating shell blasts demonstrate the impervious nature of the reinforced concrete walls. Refurbished blockhouses served as divisional and regimental CPs. Once the airfield was operational, Marine aviation units established HQ and Signals units in them. *(NARA)*

(**Opposite, below**) A Marine is shown looking for Japanese snipers in a demolished phosphate refinery at Peleliu's West Road's northern tip opposite the nearby airfield on Ngesebus-Kongauru Islands at the end of September after Marine and Army units moved north. Ngesebus Island was surrounded by a coral reef and was connected to Peleliu by a wooden causeway that was destroyed during the pre-invasion bombardment. American planners wanted to prevent the use of Ngesebus and Kongauru Islands as staging areas for Japanese reinforcements sent by General Inoue from Babelthuap or Koror further up the Palau chain. *(NARA)*

KATOWORKS
KATOWORKS
TOKYO

(**Opposite, above**) A Japanese railroad engine for Peleliu's narrow-gauge railway is shown with a Marine posing next to it. The railway was used to haul phosphate, which was one of the primary resources in the Palau Islands. An IJN insignia and 'Katoworks Tokyo' are visible at the base of the locomotive. *(NARA)*

(**Opposite, below**) A Marine is shown scanning a ridgeline for snipers near a previous Japanese MG position near the airfield. The ridges and hills that dominated the airfield below also housed Japanese artillery, which hindered the Marines' northern advance on D+1. This Marine is holding his M1911 0.45in-calibre semi-automatic pistol, a close-quarter combat weapon with excellent stopping power and a seven-round magazine. *(NARA)*

(**Above**) A Marine 0.30in-calibre Browning M1919A4 LMG crew (foreground) is shown in flat terrain near Peleliu's airfield using a limestone coral outcrop for cover to provide suppressive fire for an infantry advance on D+1. This weapon was light enough for rapid movement under fire and with its air-cooled fenestrated barrel did not require a water can. *(NARA)*

(**Above**) A Marine 0.30in-calibre, water-cooled MMG crew is shown firing their Browning M1917A1 weapon as the Japanese mount a counterattack against their unit in dense underbrush just inland from the beachhead. This weapon usually had a crew of four and had a cyclic rate of fire of 450 rounds per minute. *(NARA)*

(**Opposite, above**) A Marine bazooka team is seen here leading a column leaving the front lines after relief by 81st Division soldiers. The Marine on the far left is seen shouldering an M9 bazooka, which was a tube that fired a shaped-charge warhead at short range. Designed as an AT weapon against the treads and rear of armoured vehicles, on Peleliu it was deployed to fire its 60mm high-explosive (HE) projectile directly into Japanese caves and against reinforced MG and sniper positions. *(NARA)*

(**Opposite, below**) A white phosphorus (WP) grenade is shown exploding and emitting white smoke after it was fired at a Japanese dugout. The M15 WP grenade, which had the moniker 'Willie Pete', was originally designed for screening infantry movements. However, upon detonation, the grenade emitted white phosphorus particles which, after coming into contact with enemy soldiers' skin, would continue to burn their surface at an inordinately high temperature making it effective against enemy infantry dug into caves and the sides of ridges. The smoke and the WP made it impossible for the enemy to remain in their positions. The total weight of the M15 was just under 2lb with half of it being WP material. *(NARA)*

(**Above**) Combustible fuel from a Marine M2-2 flame-thrower is seen burning a Japanese MG nest in dense underbrush on a Peleliu ridge. The M2-2 weighed almost 70lb and entered service in 1943. The flame-thrower consisted of three tanks: two that housed 4 gallons of combustible fuel, and a third containing nitrogen propellant. Bursts of flame were fired for 8–9 seconds with a range of 70–130ft, precariously proximate for the Marine from the enemy's position. The development of flame-throwing armoured vehicles limited individual Marines using this weapon to reach remote areas (above). *(NARA)*

(**Opposite, above**) Marines are seen watching a black plume of smoke emanate from a Japanese cave at the base of a Peleliu ridge after a TNT satchel charge was detonated. Demolition teams had to be deployed when direct fire or flame-throwers were ineffective at deeply-burrowed Japanese infantry within caves, especially the tiered enemy redoubts typical of IJN construction. *(NARA)*

(**Opposite, below**) A USN Vought OS2U Kingfisher scout floatplane is shown after catapult-launching from either a cruiser or battleship. The Kingfisher was a mid-wing monoplane with a large central and two small stabilizing floats. Above the assault armada (left, background), the Kingfisher observed naval gunnery strikes on Peleliu targets. *(NARA)*

24

(**Above**) A Marine Vought F4U Corsair is shown dropping napalm on Japanese positions along one of the 'Five Sisters' with smoke from a previous Corsair sortie. Although originally designed as a USN carrier-borne aircraft, the Corsair became an excellent land-based, ground-attack fighter-bomber in the Pacific as it was armed with six 0.5in-calibre forward-firing MGs in the wings, and able to carry an external bomb or rocket load of 2,000lb. *(NARA)*

(**Opposite, above**) A USN Grumman F6F-5N Hellcat is shown on Peleliu's now operational airfield. This plane was fitted with AN/APS-6 3cm radar and two 20mm cannon in the inner wing bays and four 0.50in-calibre M2 Browning MGs in the wings, making it an excellent night-fighter. *(NARA)*

(**Opposite, below**) A Marine pilot is seen here boarding his Grumman TBF Avenger torpedo-bomber after refuelling on Peleliu. This was a three-seat carrier-borne or land-based torpedo-bomber. It had two 0.5in-calibre M2 Browning forward-firing MGs in the wings and one trainable rearward-firing 0.5in-calibre M2 Browning MG in the dorsal turret. There was also one 0.3in-calibre rearward-firing MG in the ventral position. This aircraft was capable of carrying a torpedo, bomb or rocket load of 2,500lb. *(NARA)*

F(N)59

(**Opposite, above**) Marines are shown sitting among wrecked Japanese bombers after Peleliu's airfield was captured on D+1. USN aerial bombardment neutralized both IJN and IJA air presence in the Palau Islands well before the Peleliu assault of 15 September. *(NARA)*

(**Opposite, below**) A Marine posing in front of a destroyed Japanese fighter, probably an IJN Mitsubishi A6M. The fighter plane's moniker, Zero, is derived from the Japanese name *Reisen*, which referred to the aircraft's entry year into IJN service in July 1940 that corresponded to the last digit of the Japanese Imperial year 2600. The official Allied reporting name for the fighter was Zeke. Although newer Allied aircraft were gaining parity with and even superiority over the A6M and its upgrades through to the A6M6 series, the Zero continued to serve in a front-line role until the war's end. *(NARA)*

(**Above**) A three-man Marine M2 60mm mortar crew is shown at the front line supporting the infantry's advance. This weapon weighed 42lb and fired a 3lb shell. Its maximum firing range was just over a mile. A good crew was able to fire eighteen rounds per minute maximally. Private First Class Eugene Sledge was a 60mm mortarman in K Company, 5th Marines. Sledge chronicled combat on Peleliu in his memoir *With the Old Breed.* *(NARA)*

(**Above**) A Marine M1 81mm mortar crew is shown firing a 3.1in-calibre round onto an enemy position. The mortar tube was smoothbore so the shell was stabilized by projectile tail fins. The maximal operational range of this mortar was over 3,000 yards and it could fire HE, WP, chemical smoke and illuminating shells. *(NARA)*

(**Opposite, above**) A Marine M3 37mm AT gun crew is shown firing from near a previous Japanese concrete blockhouse close to the airfield. Late on D-Day, a company-sized Japanese infantry counterattack supported by fifteen Type 95 *Ha-Go* light tanks was repulsed. The M3 AT gun, which debuted in 1937 and was obsolete by ETO standards, was effective against thin-armoured Japanese tanks and tankettes. Also the M3 37mm AT gun was used in the Pacific because of its portability on poorly-tracked islands. When firing canister or fragmenting ammunition shells, the M3 devastated Japanese infantry concentrations, performing as a 'giant shotgun'. *(NARA)*

(**Opposite, below**) An 11th Marines M8 75mm pack howitzer position is shown being readied for action against the Japanese defenders. Although developed in 1927 with the intent to give mountain troops an effective howitzer, this gun weighed only 220lb and broke down easily with re-assembly in three minutes. The metal wheels and rubber tyres aided in the positioning of this howitzer in rough terrain. *(NARA)*

(**Above**) An 11th Marines 105mm M2 A1 howitzer with its split trail gun mount is shown in action. The gun seen in the above photograph had been previously disabled by Japanese mortar fire, but was now in use again. The M2 A1 howitzer, which was produced since 1928, fired a 4.1in-calibre HE shell to a maximum range of 37,000ft and was the mainstay of the 1st Marine Division's artillery. In late 1942 on New Guinea's northern Papuan coast, the 105mm howitzer acquired a fearsome reputation as a 'bunker-buster' against Japanese reinforced fortifications that were numerous on Peleliu. *(NARA)*

(**Opposite, above**) An 11th Marines M1 155mm howitzer of the 3rd Battalion III PhibCorps Artillery is shown with its characteristic split trail gun mount. This weapon was developed in 1940 and became operational the following year. It was designed to be vehicle-transported with its HE shell maximum range being 50,000ft. *(NARA)*

(**Opposite, below**) A Marine 12th AAA Battalion 40mm Bofors gun on Peleliu is readied for any enemy aerial attack, although most Japanese air strength in the Palau Islands was neutralized before the mid-September invasion. The USN installed single, double and four-gun mounts on ships in the Pacific to combat the kamikaze attacks. On Peleliu, they were implemented as direct-firing guns aimed at Japanese caves on the numerous ridges, firing the 2lb 1.6in-calibre HE and AP shells. *(NARA)*

A Marine 12th AAA Battalion 90mm M1 AA gun mounted on the early M1 carriage is emplaced on Peleliu's coast. This gun was the primary US heavy AA gun firing a 3.5in-calibre HE shell and was ubiquitous throughout the American Pacific assaults. As enemy aerial targets dissipated over Peleliu, this gun was utilized as a conventional artillery piece against fortified ground targets, playing a similar role to the German 88mm FlaK 18 ordnance. *(NARA)*

Soldiers of the 81st Division are shown here manning a Browning M2 0.5in-calibre HMG mounted onto a jeep as they battle enemy snipers on a Peleliu ridge. This gun's cartridge had excellent penetrating ability and was useful against Japanese reinforced positions. *(NARA)*

An 81st Division soldier with his M1 0.3in-calibre carbine rifle is seen running to the front of an M3 half-track GMC mounting a 75mm gun. This vehicle saw its first deployment in North Africa where it was used as a TD. It was also used throughout the Pacific. Here, on Peleliu, it was brought into some dense vegetation at the base of an enemy-held ridge to destroy Japanese dugouts and caves. *(NARA)*

(**Above**) Several amphibious US-built DUKWs are shown moving along one of Peleliu's few roads in column on either side of the island. Appearing in 1942, the DUKW was a variant of a General Motors Corporation 6 × 6 truck with a buoyant boat-shaped hull. By the war's end, more than 21,000 DUKWs had been produced. *(NARA)*

(**Opposite, above**) An LVT(A) 4 with its M8 HMC turret housing a 75mm howitzer is shown disabled on a Peleliu landing beach on D-Day. This vehicle was to lead non-armoured amphibious tractors carrying Marines to the beaches and provide fire support with their 75mm gun prior to the arrival of M4 medium tanks. Once ashore, the LVT(A) 4 had a maximum speed of 17 mph. *(NARA)*

(**Opposite, below**) A Marine is shown inspecting the clash between an LVT(A) 4 called 'Lady Luck' with its M8 HMC turret housing a 75mm howitzer and a Japanese dual-purpose (DP) naval gun. The Japanese ordnance had its casemate in a ground-level dugout with a rock and corrugated steel roof. *(NARA)*

D12
D12

A Marine M4 medium tank, which had a bulldozer blade fitted to the front of it, is shown firing its 75mm gun up an incline at a Japanese position on a row of Peleliu's ridges during an attack by elements of the 1st Battalion, 5th Marines on 27 September (D+12). Within dense vegetation, a tank-dozer was needed to clear a path for itself to fire more effectively against the enemy. Marines behind the turret used the tank for cover as they spotted where the rounds landed for the gunner. *(NARA)*

A Marine M4 medium tank with a part of the rear wading exhaust still present is seen after its tread was destroyed by a Japanese land mine. The shallow crater from this lightweight mine is visible in the right foreground. (*NARA*)

A Marine LVT(A) with the turret of an M3 tank and its 37mm cannon is shown dwarfing a Japanese Type 95 *Ha-Go* light tank that was disabled at the beachhead after the failed enemy D-Day infantry-tank counterattack. During this attack almost all of the Japanese armour on Peleliu was lost. The *Ha-Go*, which similarly possessed a 37mm turret gun, lacked the armour penetration of the US M3 37mm AT gun. The Type 95 *Ha-Go* was one of the most numerous Japanese tanks produced, but it was vulnerable to all Marine artillery due to its thin armour. (*NARA*)

A Marine is shown de-fusing an unexploded Japanese rocket that came to rest 100ft from the airfield after it was fired from 'Suicide' (or 'Bloody Nose') Ridge. The Marines dubbed the Japanese rocket 'Screaming Mimi' or 'Whistling Willie', which was launched from pairs of narrow-gauge rails often elevated with sandbags. The rocket's characteristic noise was from the friction upon launching over the rails and the end-over-end tumbling flight. The rocket exploded with great concussive force but limited fragmentation. *(NARA)*

An improvised Japanese 40lb land mine, roughly 8in in height, is shown here. Inside this concrete device was a quart of black powder with two wires attached to externally detonate. *(NARA)*

At low tide, several different Japanese land mines are shown half-buried in the sand at one of the Marine assault beaches. As evidence of their destructive ability, along with Japanese anti-boat artillery and mortars on D-Day, are two disabled Marine vessels situated on the sand, while an LVT 4 is seen moving in the water (background). The disabled Marine amphibious vessels are a DUKW (foreground) and LVT(A) 4 behind it with its characteristic silhouette from its M8 HMC turret with a 75mm howitzer gun. *(NARA)*

(**Above**) A Marine is seen inspecting a captured Japanese Type 95 20mm automatic cannon that functioned as an AT gun in a ground-level dugout protected by rock and wood. The enemy position was well-camouflaged with ground cover from the adjacent dense underbrush. This weapon was obsolete by 1942 because of the thickness of Allied armour, like the Allied Boys AT rifle, but was effective against assault infantry and landing craft. *(NARA)*

(**Opposite, above**) A Japanese Type 96 25mm DP double-barrelled AT/AA gun is shown here in an earthen and rock emplacement. This weapon, designed by the French Hotchkiss firm, was also manufactured with single and triple barrels. This AT/AA gun had a box magazine of fifteen rounds. *(NARA)*

(**Opposite, below**) A disabled Japanese Type 41 75mm mountain gun with its large wooden wheels is shown near its coral dugout on Peleliu. This weapon fired HE, AP, hollow-charge, smoke and incendiary 75mm shells. It was originally of German design by Krupp but later manufactured at the Osaka Arsenal in Japan. It had a crew of thirteen. *(NARA)*

(**Above**) A Japanese Type 90 75mm field gun is shown in its coconut log-reinforced casemate. This artillery piece had a split trail and an armoured protective shield. Intended as a standardized 75mm field gun for the IJA, it was produced in only limited numbers. It fired the same array of 75mm rounds as the Type 41 75mm mountain gun. A good crew could fire up to fifteen rounds in a two-minute interval of sustained fire support. *(NARA)*

(**Opposite, above**) A Japanese Type 10 120mm DP gun is shown in its coral revetment after capture by American forces. Although this artillery piece was originally designed for ship use (notably IJN cruisers and escort carriers), the gun was adapted for DP land roles, AA and coastal defence. It was situated on a pedestal mount which permitted 360° of traverse. *(NARA)*

(**Opposite, below**) A captured Japanese 3rd Year 200mm Short Naval Gun for coastal defence is shown on its pedestal mount for 360° traverse in the open within a coral revetment near the shoreline. It was the primary large-calibre coastal artillery (weighing almost 4 tons) used by Japanese forces on Peleliu, having a practical firing rate of three rounds per minute. *(NARA)*

A Marine is shown gazing at a captured Japanese 3rd Year 200mm Short Naval Gun recessed in a cave with its barrel rotated inward. In addition to its open coastal defence location, the Japanese commanders on Peleliu also situated these guns in natural or hollowed-out caves. From these hidden and near-bombproof sites, Japanese gunners brought down murderous fire on the Marine D-Day assault beaches and landing craft. *(NARA)*

Chapter Three

Commanders and Combatants

Japanese Commanders

Lieutenant General Hideyoshi Obata, commander of all Central Pacific IJA units, had his 31st Army HQ on Guam. In the spring of 1944, he was briefly designated commander of the Palau Sector Group, which also included Yap and Ulithi Atolls to the Palaus' north-east in the western Caroline Islands. Tokyo ordered Obata to make the Palaus and Yap secure. Ulithi Atoll, with its fine anchorage, was not to be reinforced.

With concerns that the Palau Islands in autumn 1944 would be the next American invasion site, Tokyo reinforced Obata with the IJA 14th Division, which was en route from Manchuria to New Guinea but hastily diverted to the Palaus, reaching them on 24 April 1944. The 14th Division (with its 2nd, 15th and 59th IRs), under the command of Lieutenant General Sadae Inoue, was one of the finest IJA formations fielded. The division was activated in 1905 and was involved in the siege and capture of Port Arthur during the Russo-Japanese War. During the 1930s, the 14th Division participated in both the Manchuria and Shanghai Incidents. After garrison duty in Japan, it was moved to Manchuria in September 1940.

Inoue, commissioned in 1908 after the Russo-Japanese War, became a commanding IR colonel in 1936. After various staff officer positions in China, he was promoted to lieutenant general in 1942. The next year, he assumed command of the 14th Division. Regarded as a tenacious leader who handled adversity easily, he was not deemed a brilliant tactician.

In August 1944, as Obata's Japanese 31st Army HQ was wiped out after Guam's re-possession by US forces, Inoue was then put in charge of the Palau Sector Group, establishing his 14th Division HQ on Koror after the IJN relinquished command to him there. The Palau Sector Group was reassigned to the Japanese Southern Army headquartered in Manila. Japanese Intelligence files were captured by the Americans after their Mariana Islands' conquests revealing the Japanese Order of Battle and garrison strength on both Peleliu and Angaur. Inoue's total Palau Islands garrison strength was 35,000 troops, with an additional 8,000 to 10,000 soldiers on Yap, situated between the main Palau chain and Ulithi Atoll further to the north-east (see Map 3). He ordered the small Ulithi Atoll garrison to join his forces in the Palau

Islands. On 8 September, the Japanese Southern Army HQ warned Inoue to expect an impending attack.

Since Tokyo suspected Babelthuap, the largest Palau Island, to be invaded, Inoue stationed his heaviest concentration of troops there, approximately 25,000, including the bulk of the IJA 15th and 59th IRs. Peleliu with its important airfield was to be only defended by the IJA 2nd IR reinforced with a battalion of the 15th IR, an infantry battalion of the 53rd Independent Mixed Brigade, along with naval and other troops totalling 10,500 men, under the command of Colonel Kunio Nakagawa. Angaur had a reinforced battalion (1,500 men) of the IJA 59th IR, under Major Ushio Goto. All Japanese ground forces lacked air and naval support since the March 1944 USN carrier strikes destroyed all Peleliu-based aircraft and the IJN moved westward to safer anchorages.

Interservice rivalry between the IJA and IJN was a major problem during the Pacific campaigns, and such rivalry on Peleliu prevented an integrated defensive strategy. Colonel Nakagawa, the 2nd IR commander who arrived on Peleliu in April 1944, was one of the most able tacticians of the IJA 14th Division, especially in armoured tactics. However, on Peleliu, Nakagawa was outranked by Vice Admiral Seiichi Itō, who led the island's IJN garrison. Conflict between the two arose about the construction of defences, especially in the design of cave fortifications. Eventually, Inoue was forced to dispatch to Peleliu on 16 July his recently-arrived 14th Division infantry commander, Major General Kenjiro Murai, who was an expert on fortifications. Now Peleliu would have an IJA officer of equal rank to Vice Admiral Itō in order to intervene on behalf of Nakagawa.

Colonel Nakagawa's first priority since his Peleliu arrival was the construction of air-raid shelters either by blasting new caves or improving the natural ones. Despite Murai's presence on Peleliu, Nakagawa continued to lead the island's forces to implement a strong tactical defensive plan. Ironically Murai, the fortifications expert, argued for a last-ditch counterattack once the Americans landed, whereas Nakagawa preferred to maintain his troops in the cave and ridge defensive positions. Inoue sided with Nakagawa.

By utilizing prepared defences and bombproof shelters, Nakagawa's 2nd IR was able to survive the tremendous American naval and aerial bombardment of Peleliu. Nakagawa had no intention of conceding an uncontested beach lodgement to the Marines. He was going to make it costly for the US 1st Marine Division's assault waves on 15 September without minimizing his ability to ultimately defend Peleliu's high ground.

By the midsummer of 1944, Tokyo established a defence line further to the west of the Palaus, resulting in a reduced flow of supplies and reinforcements to Inoue for the anticipated American assault. Inoue knew that his garrisons were on their own and that Hideki Tojo, the Prime Minister and War Minister, personally instructed him and his COS, Colonel Tokuchi Tada, to fight to the death for the key Palau islands in the group.

If US forces attacked Babelthuap, Inoue's plan was to retire into the large island's interior to exact a high price in American blood. Because of his persistent notion that Babelthuap (and Koror) were the main American targets, Inoue chose not to further reinforce Nakagawa on Peleliu before the Marine invasion. In fact, Inoue only dispatched a few hundred reinforcements to Peleliu once the Marines landed. By then, it was too late to drive the entrenched 1st Marine Division back.

Japanese Troop Strength

US estimates of Japanese troop strength (10,700) on Peleliu differed from the enemy's 6,200 IJA soldiers, 3,600 naval ground (including the elite naval 45th Guard Force Detachment) and air personnel totalling 9,800 men. In fact, after the island's conquest, the count of enemy dead and captured numbered at least 11,230 men on Peleliu with, perhaps, more as scores of Japanese bodies were not recovered.

Nakagawa divided Peleliu into four defensive sectors. Major Tomita commanded the 2nd IR's 2nd Battalion of 600 men in the eastern zone. The IJA 15th IR's 3rd Battalion, led by Major Chiaki and comprising 750 troops, was situated in the southern zone. In the northern sector, Major Hiikino had 550 of the 346th Independent Infantry Battalion (of the IJA 53rd Independent Mixed Brigade). Another 600 men of the 2nd IR's 3rd Battalion were stationed in the west under the command of Captain Harada. The remainder of Nakagawa's troops were in prepared defensive positions in Peleliu's high ground.

The Japanese were not prepared to relinquish any Peleliu sector without tenacious defence. Inoue, who survived the war and subsequent war crimes trials, recounted during post-war interrogation that Japanese infantry were initially to repel the Peleliu invasion with counterattacks from prepared positions along the beaches and destroy the American assault waves at the water's edge. Ultimately, Inoue agreed with the more junior Nakagawa to offer resistance at the beaches, but not mount any major counterattack on the Marine beaches.

On the ridges of Peleliu's Umurbrogol Mountain, the Japanese artillery battalion was deployed to shell the Marine landing areas. Colonel Nakagawa's tank company was to be held in the island's centre in order to mount local counterattacks against any threatening Marine inland advance.

On Angaur, the Japanese had only the 1st Battalion, 59th IR of approximately 1,400 men, under Major Goto, to resist the US 81st Division's two-regiment attack. Inoue ordered Colonel Eguchi and his two other 59th IR battalions along with support troops back to Koror in July 1944 for the defence of Babelthuap against a feared American assault there. Thus US planners overestimated Japanese strength on Angaur, believing that there was an additional IJA force totalling 2,500 to 3,000 there.

The Japanese defences on Peleliu and Angaur were first tested on 12 September when the massive pre-invasion American naval and air bombardment commenced.

American Commanders

Admiral Chester W. Nimitz was C-in-C, Pacific Fleet (CINCPAC) and C-in-C Pacific Ocean Area (CINCPOA). He was in overall command of Operation STALEMATE II and it was his final decision that unleashed the invasion of Peleliu and Angaur as well as Ulithi Atoll.

Admiral Halsey assumed control over all Central Pacific operations as commander of the USN's Third Fleet. Task Force (TF) 31, which was responsible for carrying and unloading the expeditionary force at Peleliu and Angaur, was under the command of Vice Admiral Thomas Wilkinson, who succeeded Vice Admiral Richmond Kelly Turner in August 1943 as commander of the Third Amphibious Force. The Heavy Striking Force (TF34) consisting of older battleships and heavy cruisers was commanded by Rear Admiral Jesse Oldendorf. The Light Striking Force (TF35) was commanded by Rear Admiral W.L. Ainsworth. The large fleet carriers of TF38 were led by Rear Admiral William Sample, while escort carriers were commanded by Rear Admiral Ralph Ofstie.

Marine Major General Roy S. Geiger commanded IIIAC. Geiger's earlier career was Marine Corps aviation and he led the 1st MAW on Guadalcanal. After a brief tour as Director of Marine Corps Aviation, he assumed command of IMAC on Bougainville from Lieutenant General Alexander Vandegrift, who became Marine Corps Commandant. IMAC was renamed IIIAC on 15 April 1944. Geiger, although an aviator, was well-respected as a ground commander by both Admirals Nimitz and Halsey.

Major Generals William H. Rupertus and Paul J. Mueller commanded 1st Marine Division and the Army's 81st Infantry ('Wildcats') Division respectively. Rupertus had commanded the 1st Battalion, 4th Marines in Shanghai during the Japanese occupation of the city in 1937. Unfortunately, while in China, Rupertus' wife and two children died during an epidemic there. At Guadalcanal, he was a brigadier general and served as the 1st Marine Division's Assistant Division Commander (ADC) under Vandegrift. He became permanent commander of the division on 8 July 1943, in charge of planning the New Britain campaign under MacArthur's leadership. The combat on New Britain was fierce, along with debilitating weather conditions and diseases.

The 1st Marine Division ('The Old Breed') acquired before Peleliu a reputation as being the Corps' premier division with an illustrious Pacific campaign history including Guadalcanal in the Solomon Islands as well as at Cape Gloucester and the Willaumez Peninsula on New Britain in the Bismarck Archipelago. In May 1944, Nimitz recalled the 1st Division from New Britain to Pavuvu, the largest of the Russell Islands in the Solomon chain, to receive almost 5,000 replacements. Nimitz wanted it back from MacArthur for future CPA amphibious operations. Rupertus broke his ankle during the pre-invasion amphibious training on Pavuvu and utilized a cane while on Peleliu. He concealed his injury from his superiors, fearing his removal from divisional command. The ankle fracture may have contributed to his assumption of direct command on the beach at Peleliu on D+1.

Rupertus had Brigadier General Oliver P. Smith as his ADC. Prior to the war, Smith had a number of staff and instructor assignments before being ordered to the Pacific after commanding the 1st Battalion, 6th Marines in Iceland in 1940–41. Smith served as a battalion commander on Guadalcanal and as the 5th Marines' regimental commander on New Britain during the Talasea operations on the Willaumez Peninsula. On D-Day, it was Smith who went to supervise the Peleliu beachhead, which was by no means secure.

Colonel John T. Selden was the 1st Marine Division's COS. Regimental commanders for the Peleliu operation were Colonels Lewis B. 'Chesty' Puller (1st Marines), Herman H. Hanneken (7th Marines) and Harold D. Harris (5th Marines). Puller and Hanneken were veteran battalion commanders on Guadalcanal, with earlier experience in the Caribbean campaigns on Haiti and in Nicaragua in the 1930s.

Colonel Puller disliked Japanese soldiery dating back to Shanghai in 1933, where he commanded a Horse Marine detachment. In 1940, he confronted a Japanese unit commanded by an IJA colonel dispatched to forcibly abduct Chinese workers from a US Marine-protected zone. On Guadalcanal, Puller received his third Navy Cross as a lieutenant colonel commanding the 1st Battalion, 7th Marines. Puller was promoted to command the 1st Marines on 22 February 1944 after his service on New Britain.

Colonel Hanneken was a Congressional Medal of Honor recipient for his gallantry in the pre-Second World War Haiti campaign, where he infiltrated rebel defences and killed their leader, Charlemagne Péralte, at his HQ. In Nicaragua in 1929, Hanneken captured one of César Sandino's rebel associates and received a Navy Cross for killing another rebel leader. On Guadalcanal, Hanneken commanded the 2nd Battalion, 7th Marines. On New Britain, Hanneken was COS to the division's ADC prior to being given the command of the 7th Marines in February 1944.

Colonel Harris, commander of the 5th Marines, also had combat and leadership roles on New Britain. Unlike Puller and Hanneken, Harris was commissioned upon US Naval Academy graduation. He did a tour in the mid-1930s at the prestigious US Army's Infantry School at Fort Benning, Georgia. Harris, too, saw overseas service in China and Nicaragua. He served as Executive Officer, 1st Marines on New Britain and in February 1944 as Divisional Assistant COS, Intelligence prior to receiving command of the 5th Marines just before Peleliu.

Colonel William H. Harrison commanded the 11th Marines' artillery units on Peleliu, which had a superb reputation from the Guadalcanal campaign. Harrison was a junior officer in France at the end of the First World War's hostilities. He served in the Haitian and Dominican campaigns during the interwar years before gaining artillery experience at the Field Artillery School at Fort Sill, Oklahoma. Prior to Pearl Harbor, he was with the 10th Marine Artillery Regiment. After the Japanese attack, he commanded the Marine 12th Defence Battalion in California, prior to departure to Samoa and then Australia. He served on the unoccupied Woodlark Island, located in the Solomon Sea between the eastern tip of New Guinea and Bougainville, prior to leading his battalion at Cape Gloucester, New Britain. He was appointed commander of the 11th Marines for the Peleliu invasion in 1944.

The US Army's 81st Infantry ('Wildcats') Division's commanding general was Major General Paul J. Mueller, who took over the division in August 1942. A majority of the division's officers (as well as Mueller) were new to combat. The 81st was a regular division with its soldiers coming from mainly the Midwest and southern United States. It comprised the 321st, 322nd and 323rd IRs. Peleliu, Angaur and Ulithi Atoll would be their initial combat experience.

The 81st Division left Oahu's Schofield Barracks on 11 August 1944 and arrived on Guadalcanal for practice amphibious runs on 24 August. The 81st divisional staff and planners focused for their primary objective the invasion of Angaur. In actuality, the 81st Division's three IRs were initially a floating reserve for the Peleliu invasion; however, senior Marine commanders did not request Army reinforcements during the first days of fierce island combat.

As for the Angaur assault, the Japanese did not have any permanent military installations there. As Army Intelligence upgraded Angaur's garrison strength from 300 enemy soldiers to a reinforced regiment, two of the 81st's IRs were to make the attack on 17 September, the 322nd and 321st RCTs under the commands of Colonel Benjamin Venable (landing at Red Beach on the north-east coast) and Colonel Robert Dark (landing at Blue Beach on the south-east coast).

By 16 September, Admiral Wilkinson received a directive from Admiral Halsey to take the many islands in Ulithi Atoll to the northeast of Yap Atoll, with the third RCT of the 81st Division, the 323rd. The American planners erred in the commitment of the entire 323rd RCT as there were no Japanese at Ulithi. With two RCTs of the 81st attacking Angaur with its enemy garrison of only 1,400 men and a third RCT assaulting the non-occupied islands in the Ulithi Atoll, the 1st Marine Division had landed on Peleliu without impressive numerical superiority, thereby forcing the Marines to utilize service personnel in combat roles in order to maintain the initial momentum after the 15 September landings.

Admiral Chester W. Nimitz, CINCPAC and CINCPOA (centre), is shown inspecting Namur Island in Kwajalein Atoll after its seizure in the Marshall Islands in February 1944. His controversial decision to invade Peleliu and Angaur was based on a fear that the Japanese bombers based on Peleliu posed a risk to MacArthur's proposed invasion of Mindanao 500 miles east of the Palau Islands. Japanese air power in the Palaus was neutralized in March 1944, raising an alternative scenario by US Third Fleet commander, Admiral William F. Halsey Jr, of simply bypassing Peleliu and the other Palau Islands. However, Nimitz prevailed with JCS approval to assault the Palaus in September 1944. Nimitz hoped to acquire airfields and fleet anchorage on Peleliu and Ulithi Atoll, respectively, for further CPA advances without much bloodshed. *(NARA)*

(**Above**) Secretary of the Navy James Forrestal (front row, left), Major General Harry Schmidt CG 4th Marine Division (back row, left) and Admiral Raymond A. Spruance, commander Central Pacific Force (re-designated US Fifth Fleet in April 1944) on a jeep tour of Namur Island in Kwajalein Atoll in the Marshall Islands after their capture in February 1944. Spruance adroitly commanded the American invasion and secured numerous airfields in the CPA north-western advance. *(NARA)*

(**Opposite, above**) American commanders are shown on Angaur after that island's expeditious capture. In the front row, from left to right, are shown Major General Roy S. Geiger, IIIAC commander; Admiral Halsey, commander of the US Third Fleet; Major General Paul J. Mueller, commanding general of the US 81st Infantry Division *(NARA)*

(**Opposite, below**) The 1st Marine Division commanding general, Major General William H. Rupertus (left) and Assistant Division commander, Brigadier General Oliver P. Smith are shown in a makeshift CP. Rupertus did not land on D-Day, probably due to a concealed ankle fracture sustained during the Pavuvu Island amphibious training. At 1130 hours on D-Day, Smith came ashore with a skeleton staff and set up an advance CP in an overrun AT ditch just inland from Orange Beach 2. Being situated in the reverse bank of this sharp decline, the division's CP had excellent protection from the near-constant enemy shelling. *(NARA)*

Major General Rupertus is shown in the front row (centre), holding his cane necessitated by an ankle fracture. With him, in front of his divisional CP after 24 September, are his staff officers: in the front row (left to right) are USN Captain Logue and Marine Colonel John T. Selden, the division's COS. In the back row (left to right) are Marine Lieutenant Colonels Harvey C. Tschirgi (G-4, Logistics), Lewis J. Fields (G-3, Operations), Harold O. Deakin (G-1, Personnel) and John W. Scott (G-2, Intelligence). *(NARA)*

Company M's 1st Lieutenant Lewis B. Puller (second from left) is shown with his Gunnery Sergeant William Lee (second from right). They are flanked by Nicaraguan National Guardsmen in 1931 during an insurgency there. Many notable Marine officers including Vandegrift, Puller and Hanneken served during those conflicts, gaining valuable training in jungle terrain and tactics. *(NARA)*

(**Opposite, above**) A 4th Marines 0.30in-calibre MG is shown in its sandbagged emplacement with surrounding Marines in Shanghai in 1937 at the intersection of Gordon and Inchan Roads. Both Rupertus and Puller served as 'China Marines' during the 1930s and witnessed some of the IJA brutality against Chinese civilians. *(NARA)*

(**Opposite, below**) A shirtless Colonel Lewis 'Chesty' Puller is shown shaking hands with Admiral Edward L. Cochrane, Chief of the Bureau of Ships, at an advanced 1st Marines CP during the latter's visit to Peleliu. In addition to service in Nicaragua, Haiti and Shanghai, Puller won a third Navy Cross for his valour and leadership as a 7th Marines' battalion commander on Guadalcanal. *(NARA)*

(**Above**) Colonel Herman H. Hanneken (left foreground), who commanded the 7th Marines on Peleliu, is shown here surveying a potential regimental CP. On Guadalcanal, Hanneken commanded the 2nd Battalion, 7th Marines and was given command of the 7th Marines after an assignment as COS to the Assistant Divisional Commander. Among his men, like Puller, he was highly regarded for his fearlessness. *(NARA)*

Colonel Harold D. 'Bucky' Harris (right), commander of the 5th Marines, is shown walking from the CP with the division's commander, Major General William Rupertus. Harris was younger than Puller and Hanneken, and unlike them was an Annapolis graduate (Class of 1925) and a student at many staff colleges. Like his two other regimental commanders, he did service in China and Nicaragua, but had not seen combat on Guadalcanal. After serving with the 1st Marines in New Britain, Harris was given the new command of the 5th Marines just before Peleliu's invasion. *(NARA)*

Colonel William H. Harrison (far left), commander of the 11th Marines (Artillery) is shown with the division's G-2, Colonel John Scott (second from left). In the middle is the division's Assistant Commander, Brigadier General Oliver P. Smith. All are standing near a captured Japanese 150mm mortar. *(NARA)*

Marine Lieutenant Colonel Joslyn R. Bailey, commanding officer of MAG 11, leaves his office in a wrecked, previous Japanese blockhouse near the airfield at the southern end of Peleliu. Bailey worked closely with the 5th Marines battalion and regimental commanders to provide tactical air support for Marine and Army units against the last-ditch Japanese defenders within the multitude of mutually-defended enemy positions in the 'Umurbrogol Pocket' during October 1944. *(NARA)*

Lieutenant Colonel Robert G. Balance, commander of the 1st Marine Division's Shore Party Group, is shown on a field telephone at an assault beach near his CP. He led the 1st Pioneer Battalion against the enemy on D-Day, despite being wounded in the face by shrapnel. *(NARA)*

Marine Lieutenant Colonel Austin C. Shofner, 3rd Battalion, 5th Marines CO, is shown here holding a field telephone in his left hand and his M1 carbine in his right one. Shofner was one of the few Marine officers who escaped from Japanese prison confinement in the Philippines after the fall of Corregidor in May 1942. During the first few minutes of the D-Day assault, Shofner lost his Executive Officer (XO) Major Robert Ash, who was killed by a Japanese artillery shell. The LVT carrying the 3rd Battalion's communications equipment and signallers was also destroyed on the reef. On the night of D-Day, Shofner was wounded by an enemy mortar round and his battalion was taken over throughout the night by Lieutenant Colonel Lewis W. Walt, XO 5th Marines, until Major John H. Gustafson, who was XO 2nd Battalion, 5th Marines during the assault, became the official battalion commander. On 3 October, after recovering from his wounds, Shofner took over as CO, Division HQ Battalion. *(NARA)*

(**Above, left**) Lieutenant Colonel Robert W. Boyd, CO, 1st Battalion, 5th Marines is shown holding a field telephone in a shell hole that was functioning as his CP on D+1. On D-Day, Boyd's battalion along with Lieutenant Colonel Honsowetz's 2nd Battalion, 1st Marines was at the centre of a major Japanese tank-infantry counterattack that began to develop at 1600 hours. Colonel Harris ordered that both of his 5th Marines' assault battalions land with their 37mm AT guns and heavy MGs in order to emplace them in forward positions as soon as possible. Boyd also deployed three M4 medium tanks in a partial defilade position to place 75mm turret gunfire to the front of the charging Japanese infantry. *(NARA)*

(**Above, right**) Lieutenant Colonel Spencer S. Berger, CO, 2nd Battalion, 7th Marines, is shown holding a field telephone at his impromptu CP on 'Suicide Ridge' late during the battle for Peleliu amid fanatical Japanese resistance on the island's high ground to the north-west. On D-Day, Berger commanded the same battalion as the divisional reserve, when General Rupertus unilaterally decided to send this unit into the combat fray to add punch to Hanneken's troops that had become mired in an inland swamp. Between 1500 and 1600 hours, Berger was ordered to find any available LCVPs and load up his men from transports for transit to the transfer line at the coral reef's edge. This movement deteriorated at the transfer line since there was no USN control officer who knew how to land the Marines in LVTs. Trying to move across the reef with the boats he had as darkness was approaching, his force attracted heavy sporadic Japanese artillery fire and Berger was ordered back to his transport, the *Leedstown*. After rounding up his seasick Marines for a night on the transport, Berger landed his battalion on Peleliu at 0800 hours on D+1 roughly fifteen hours after he had been originally ordered to disembark. *(NARA)*

Major Lloyd W. Martin (right) and PFC William F. Langer, both Pennsylvanians, are seen here going over map coordinates for a fire mission at a 7th Marines CP. Both Marines were veterans of Guadalcanal and Cape Gloucester. Martin was third in command (Bn-3) of his regiment's 1st Battalion. *(NARA)*

Marine Second Lieutenant Jack Dearmore (right), a veteran of Guadalcanal and Cape Gloucester, is shown surveying a gun position. Once ashore, the 11th Marines artillery was crucial to neutralizing enemy fortifications in the caves and ridges along Umurbrogol Mountain. *(NARA)*

Marine Second Lieutenant William B. Gramley is shown spotting as a forward artillery observer for a battery of the 11th Marines 155mm howitzers. These guns had shown their efficacy at destroying log and concrete-reinforced bunkers in previous Pacific campaigns and were now vital in neutralizing the well-constructed enemy fortifications on Peleliu. *(NARA)*

Lieutenant General Sadae Inoue is shown signing the instrument of surrender for the unoccupied Palau Island Group with HQ on Koror to Marine Brigadier General F.O. Rogers, CG on Peleliu, aboard the USS *Amick*, a destroyer escort on 2 September 1945. Inoue also commanded the IJA 14th Division that was dispatched from Manchuria to the Palau Islands in early 1944. In transit from Manchuria to the Palaus, Inoue met with the prime minister and War Minister Hideki Tojo in Tokyo, where Japan's military leader emphasized that all the key islands in the Palau Group were to be defended to the death. *(NARA)*

(**Left**) Vice Admiral Seiichi Itō, the CO of the IJN air unit on Peleliu is shown here. He commanded the Palau Island Group before Inoue's arrival with the IJA 14th Division in April 1944. For more than a year before the IJA 14th Division's 2nd IR arrived, Itō's 214th Naval Construction Battalion had been busy constructing underground caves to serve as air-raid shelters, living areas and supply depots, mostly on the north-western peninsula of Peleliu with the most extensively-constructed ridgeline fortifications under the peaks of the 'Five Brothers'. *(NARA)*

(**Right**) Lieutenant Colonel Kunio Nakagawa, commander of the 14th Division's 2nd IR (Reinforced), was sent by Inoue to establish the defences on Peleliu to resist an American amphibious operation. Interservice rivalry and design of cave defences plus other matters erupted between Itō and Nakagawa. To mitigate the squabbling, as Itō outranked Nakagawa, Inoue dispatched Major General Kenjiro Murai, the 14th Division's infantry commander and an expert on fortifications to Peleliu in mid-July 1944. After the battle, it was determined that both Nakagawa and Murai died. *(NARA)*

A Japanese soldier is shown at the instant of hurling a 'Bangalore torpedo' at an approaching Marine M4 medium tank. This weapon, devised in 1912, contained an explosive charge placed within one or several connected tubes to clear obstacles. However, it was commonplace for Japanese soldiers to suicidally rush American armour with a variety of weapons including TNT satchels, mines and hand grenades, especially when there was insufficient accompanying American infantry to protect the tanks. *(NARA)*

(**Opposite, above**) The charred corpses of Japanese riflemen from the 1st Battalion, 2nd IR that were riding the backs of Type 95 *Ha-Go* medium tanks of the IJA 14th Division Tank Company are seen here after the D-Day enemy counterattack. The Japanese armour raced ahead of the remaining accompanying enemy infantry. Marine AT guns, artillery, M4 medium tanks and half-track mounted ordnance decimated the late-afternoon armour-infantry attack that was launched from north of the airfield into the 5th Marines sector. *(NARA)*

(**Above**) The corpses of Japanese artillerymen manning their 75mm gun are inspected by Marines along a track partially obscured by dense brush on either side. Colonel Nakagawa had at least one battalion of 75mm artillery in addition to several 81 and 150mm mortars. The IJA 14th Army's artillery and mortar strength was below authorized strength due to losses in transit to the Palaus or destroyed on Saipan. *(NARA)*

(**Opposite, below**) A Japanese sniper is shown dead at the base of a palm tree from which he was shot. Ubiquitous enemy tactics included infiltration, sniping and small group suicidal rushes of Marine positions. *(NARA)*

(**Above**) A Marine killed by a Japanese sniper on the front lines is lowered from his position by three of his comrades. A rifle grenade-launcher is shown in the foreground and was used effectively at isolated enemy positions along the ridges and caves of Peleliu. The rifle grenade was a standard Mk II hand grenade clipped to a firing tube, which fitted over the rifle attachment and was launched by a powerful blank cartridge. *(NARA)*

(**Opposite, above**) Two Marine Intelligence officers (left) and a Nisei interpreter (far right) are shown instructing a Japanese PoW where other enemy soldiers were holding out. When the Japanese PoW approached his comrades to coax them to surrender, he was shot dead by one of his own. This Nisei soldier was attached to the Marines as part of the Allied Translator and Interpreter Service that began in early 1943. *(NARA)*

(**Opposite, below**) Six Japanese PoWs are shown seated while another was litter-borne surrounded by a group of Marines. The Japanese had attempted to swim off Peleliu, but they were captured by an American amphibious tractor that brought them to shore. *(NARA)*

(**Above, left**) A 1st Marine Division rifleman on Peleliu is shown with a face full of anguish during combat on the island. In addition to a tenacious, well-dug-in foe, the American Marines and soldiers faced stifling heat, humidity and thirst. *(NARA)*

(**Above, right**) A soldier from the US 81st Division is shown getting a rest in the action on Angaur during which two American RCTs quickly overwhelmed the enemy battalion-strength garrison there. The two Army regiments were then transferred to Peleliu to assist the Marines in their northward advance and assault on the 'Umurbrogol Pocket'. *(NARA)*

(**Right**) An African-American Marine of the 11th Marine Depot Company attached to the 1st Marine Division as an SB is shown during a lull in the combat on Peleliu. Due to a shortage of Marine riflemen early in the campaign, many of the African-American Marine SBs and service troops assumed a combat role. Seventeen men from this company were wounded during the Peleliu campaign. Major General William H. Rupertus wrote a commendation to these African-American Marines for their gallantry. Breaking a 167-year interval, the Marine Corps began enlisting African-Americans on 1 June 1942 following an executive order by President Roosevelt. Training for 1,200 volunteers commenced for the members of the 51st Composite Defence Battalion at Camp Lejeune's Montford Point at New River, North Carolina. *(NARA)*

Marines are seen here struggling up a steep, rocky ridge to bring ammunition and water to their front-line comrades. Note the 'jerry can' filled with water behind the Marine in the background. Water was scarce on the island as Marines and soldiers fought in tropical heat and humidity. *(NARA)*

A USN Corpsman is shown tending to a wounded Marine amid Peleliu's dense underbrush. Insignia or Red Cross armbands were often not worn by corpsmen or medics to avoid becoming prized targets for Japanese snipers. *(NARA)*

A wounded 81st Division soldier is shown receiving a plasma infusion on Angaur during the intense but brief combat on that island to the south of Peleliu. Among the assaulting infantrymen of the 321st and 322nd IRs, the Americans suffered 260 killed and more than 1,350 wounded. Virtually all the 1,400 Japanese defenders were killed on Angaur, with 50 PoWs taken. *(NARA)*

A Marine PFC is shown removing a fuse from a Japanese mine planted to resist the beach assault. This mine was most likely a Model 96 that was capable of being used on land or under water. This type was typically 20in diameter and had a total weight of 107lb. It packed 46lb of explosive and was primarily implemented to thwart American assault craft on the beach and making their run to the shore. *(NARA)*

Four 11th Marines are shown carrying tubes of ammunition from a sandbagged ammunition dump (right background) for their 75mm pack howitzers to the front lines. These versatile, relatively lightweight guns could be quickly broken down and moved to the front lines when needed or fired from fixed batteries. *(NARA)*

(**Above**) The three crewmen of a USN Grumman TBF Avenger torpedo-bomber, commanded by Lieutenant Clark Miller (left), are shown standing by their aircraft after it was forced to land at the Peleliu airfield after running out of fuel. This was the first American aircraft to land at the recently-captured airfield. The Avenger saw its combat debut in a disastrous way at the Battle of Midway in June 1942, where many were decimated by Japanese fighters and IJN AA fire during their low-altitude torpedo attacks. During later years, the Avenger proved to be a workhorse of the USN carrier groups and Marine Corps aviation wings. *(NARA)*

(**Opposite, above**) A Marine Corps Corsair ground crew is shown loading a 165lb auxiliary fuel tank under the plane's fuselage. The Corsair, with its characteristic 'gull-shaped' wings was an extremely versatile fighter-bomber that could be either land-based or carrier-borne. The aircraft delivered bombs, napalm, rockets and strafing MG fire onto enemy positions in support of American infantry. *(NARA)*

(**Opposite, below**) Marine Corps Corsair pilots and ground crewmen are shown before a mission at the hard-won, X-shaped Peleliu airstrip. The auxiliary fuel tank was needed to give the Corsair more time in the air to circle over targets and coordinate attacks with ground controllers. *(NARA)*

179
179

A Marine radioman is shown racing across the beachhead with his portable radio transceiver communications unit on D-Day. The device was a Signal Corps Radio (SCR)-300 backpack radio with telephone handset which was labelled the first 'walkie-talkie' and was accepted by the War Department in the spring of 1942. Also developed later that year was the first hand-held 'walkie-talkie' device, the SCR-536, introduced for company-platoon communications. The SCR-300 first saw action in the Pacific during the New Georgia campaign in the Solomon Islands in 1943. Keeping the batteries fresh and non-corroded in the wet tropical climate was the major difficulty; otherwise, they were excellent for front-line communication. *(NARA)*

Marine Lieutenant Colonel H. Ramsey (standing), the 1st Marine Division's Signals Officer, is shown on 29 September with his men in the Communications Room at Divisional HQ at a captured Japanese airfield's administration building. *(NARA)*

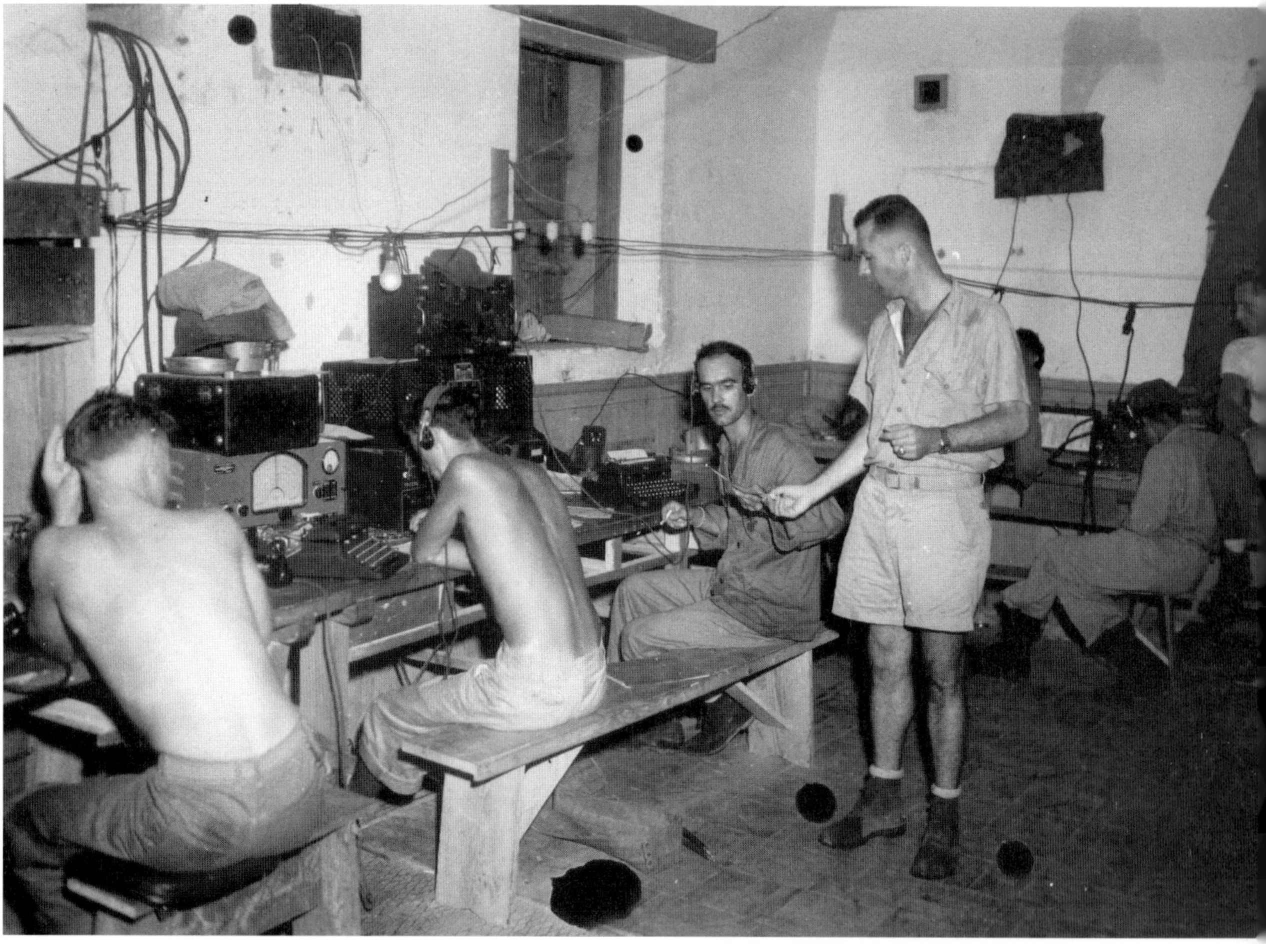

A pair of Marines, with their SCR set lying on the ground (left), is shown amid some dense vegetation. The two Marines were functioning as advanced forward artillery spotters and were calling in target corrections. *(NARA)*

An 11th Marines Fire Direction team is shown at a mapping table in a sandbagged redoubt. The Marine (left) is shown holding a telephone and receiving coordinate corrections from forward observers for their 105mm howitzer fire missions. *(NARA)*

USN Seaman Second Class Kenneth Miles is seen here passing coordinates with his SCR to his destroyer for the ship's 5in gun batteries' fire missions. These guns were useful in firing from offshore at Japanese ridge and cave positions. *(NARA)*

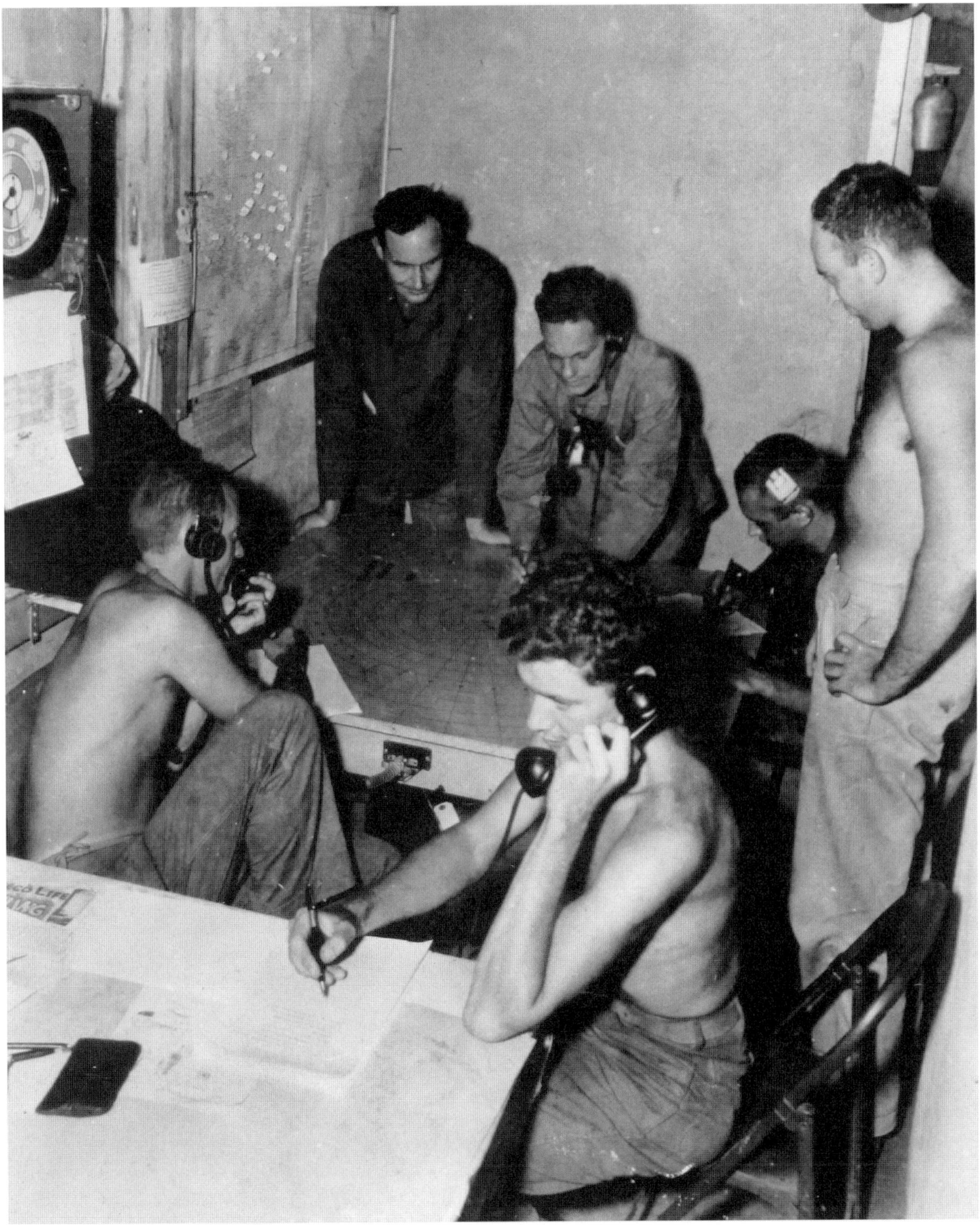

The 7th AAA Battalion Command Post on Angaur is shown in operation shortly after that island's invasion. By this stage of the war, the Japanese air presence in the Palau Island Group had been crippled by USN carrier strikes in the preceding months. AAA guns were still used as heavier-calibre artillery weapons against Japanese strongpoints. (*NARA*)

(**Above**) The five-man crew of an M4 medium tank attached to the 81st Division on Peleliu is shown here. American armour with the 75mm turret guns that could fire HE and WP shells was vital to assist the infantry in combating dug-in enemy fortifications that possessed too many Japanese MGs to attack solely with hand grenades, bazookas or TNT satchels across terrain without cover. *(NARA)*

(**Opposite, above**) Exhausted 81st Division soldiers are shown resting near 'Bloody Gulch' along the narrow gauge railway on 23 September after seven days of near-constant combat on Angaur. *(NARA)*

(**Opposite, below**) Marine riflemen PFCs Don Bloodgood and Walter McHugh are shown with their German Shepherd dog taking cover behind a concrete wall after receiving Japanese fire. These Marines were part of the 4th War Dog Platoon. The canines, which included Doberman Pinschers, carried messages, searched out hidden enemy positions and served as 'lookouts' against Japanese infiltration of Marine lines after picking up the scent of enemy soldiers. *(NARA)*

Soldiers of the 81st Division are shown getting their food behind the shelter of a Marine LVT(A) 4, which mounted an M8 75mm HMC turret and a 0.50in-calibre HMG. *(NARA)*

Chapter Four

American IIIAC Landings on Peleliu, Angaur and Ulithi

1st Marine Division's D-Day Assault

Halsey's Third Fleet covered the landing of Geiger's III Amphibious Corps (IIIAC), comprising the 1st Marine and the Army's 81st Infantry Divisions assaulting Peleliu on 15 September and Angaur on 17 September 1944. At Peleliu, a three-day naval and aerial bombardment softened up Japanese defences there. On D-Day at Peleliu, direct naval supporting fire commenced at 0800 hours with HE shells to destroy enemy beach fortifications and WP smoke to block out Japanese observation from high ground north of the airfield.

Almost 100 USN carrier-borne fighter-bombers in two divided flights strafed and bombed enemy targets proximate to the beaches. Additionally, the two additional types of naval vessels preceded the first assault waves, comprising eighteen LCI (Gun) equipped with 4.5in rocket-launchers and four LCI (Mortar) armed with three 4.2in mortars.

Prior 1st Marine Division amphibious landings at Guadalcanal and Cape Gloucester met with little Japanese opposition due to tactical surprise. The initial Marine assault waves followed the 3rd Armoured Amphibian Battalion's LVT(A)s towards the landing beaches as naval gunfire landed more forward and laterally. The LVT(A)s were specially-designed amphibious tractors with additional armour and either a turreted 37mm, the LVT(A) 1, or a 75mm howitzer, called the LVT(A) 4, to act as traditional tanks to suppress Japanese beach defences for the initial assault waves.

Japanese artillery opened up when the Marine LCVPs reached the transfer line to board amphibious tractors (LVT 2s and LVT 4s) at the edge of the coral reef for the trip to the shore. Enemy gunfire set several DUKWs and amphibian tractors ablaze along the reef. Nonetheless, the LVT(A)s reached the shore, which the enemy had mined, at 0830 hours. Japanese infantry remained inland except for a limited, scattered presence. Marine M4 medium tanks soon arrived in subsequent waves to take over from the thinner-armoured amphibious tractors; however, several of these were disabled or knocked out by Japanese artillery situated atop Peleliu's south-east promontory. As amphibious tractors were destroyed, there were fewer to return to

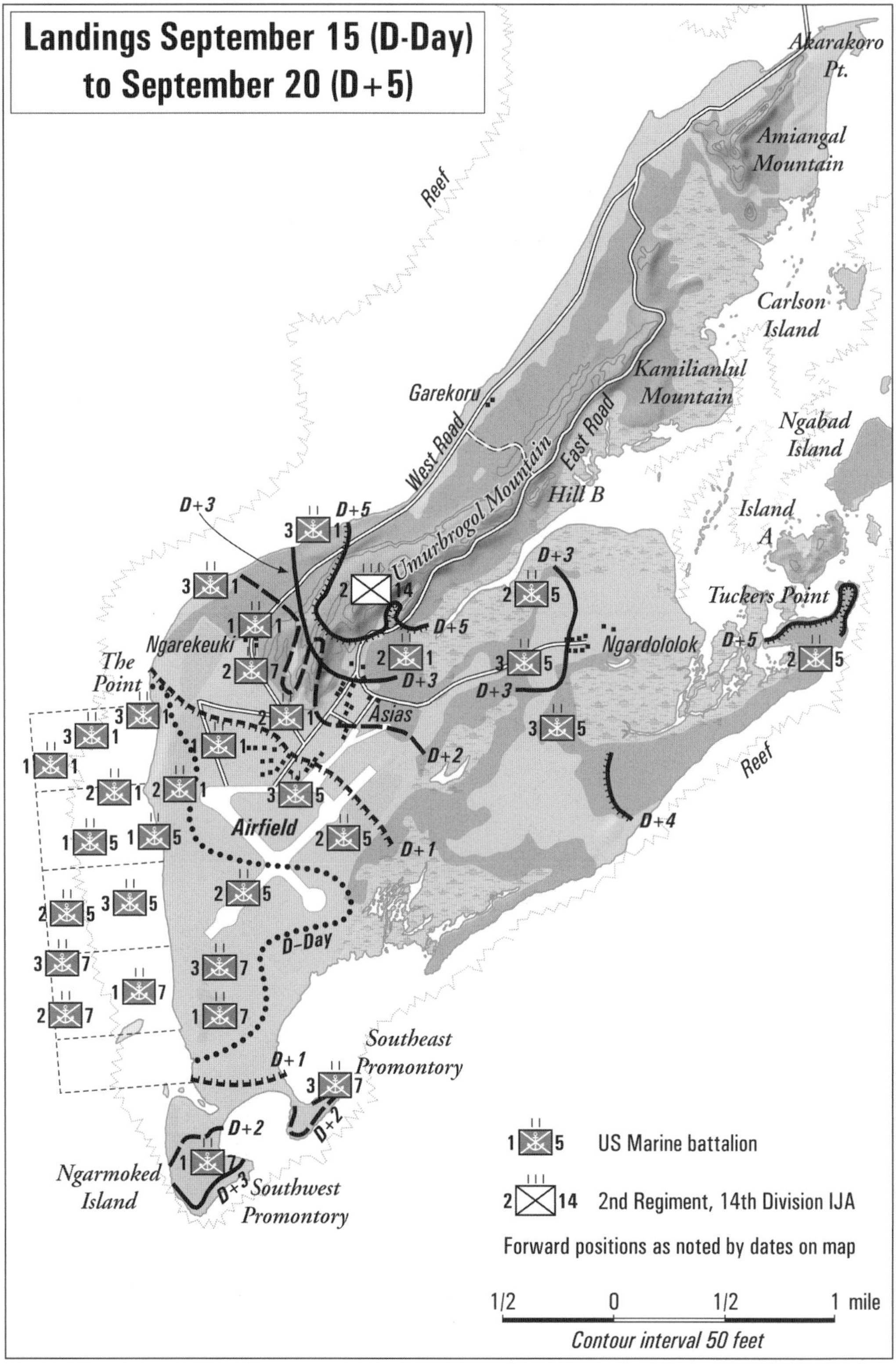

Landings September 15 (D-Day) to September 20 (D+5)
Akarakoro Pt.
Amiangal Mountain
Reef
Carlson Island
Kamilianlul Mountain
Garekoru
West Road
East Road
Ngabad Island
Umurbrogol Mountain
Hill B
Island A
Tuckers Point
Ngarekeuki
The Point
Ngardololok
Asias
Airfield
D-Day
Southeast Promontory
Ngarmoked Island
Southwest Promontory
US Marine battalion
2nd Regiment, 14th Division IJA
Forward positions as noted by dates on map
1/2 0 1/2 1 mile
Contour interval 50 feet

the reef's transfer line and subsequent assault waves' formation at the coral's edge was delayed. The Japanese resistance at the landing beaches was more vigorous than anticipated, resulting in a high percentage of Marines and vehicles lost at the shoreline. Twenty-six amphibious tractors were destroyed on D-Day.

The 1st Marines, under Puller, were assigned to assault the far left (northernmost) White Beaches 1 and 2 with the 3rd and 2nd Battalions landing at those respective sites at 0830 hours. The 1st Battalion, 1st Marines was the regimental reserve and landed between the two battalions at 0945 hours. There was 'moderate' Japanese resistance at White Beach 2 and the 2nd Battalion reached a point 350 yards inland through dense woods.

At White Beach 1, the 3rd Battalion, 1st Marines faced tenacious Japanese small-arms fire and artillery/mortar fire straddling the shoreline. Five LVTs carrying Puller's command group had been hit crossing the reef, which led to losses in communications equipment and signallers. A 30ft tall coral ridge at the extreme left (north) of the divisional front, which was not previously identified on Marine maps, was a warren of dug-in defensive positions carved into the rock and reinforced with steel or concrete. This enemy-entrenched site, called 'The Point', resisted the 3rd Battalion's initial frontal attack, even when supported with Marine tanks. Subsequent assaults on these Japanese fortifications from the rear over the next few hours were successful in reducing the blockhouses, one of which contained a 47mm AT/anti-boat cannon built into the coral that was raking and blasting the beach since the 3rd Battalion landed. Marine Captain George P. Hunt led his men from Company K in this most lethal action and narrowly held on to 'The Point' with less than a score of Marines. Approximately two-thirds of Company K was lost in one of the most deadly actions of the island war in the Pacific. The reserve 1st Battalion was committed to assist the 3rd Battalion on D-Day.

Orange Beaches 1 and 2, in the centre of the 1st Marine Division's amphibious assault, were to be attacked by Harris's 5th Marines. The 1st Battalion, 5th Marines landed at Orange Beach 1, while the 3rd Battalion came ashore at Orange Beach 2 at

---

Map 7. Landings from 15–20 September (D-Day to D+5). After transferring from LCVPs to amphibian tractors at the coral reef's edge, on 15 September (D-Day), the 1st Marines assaulted White 1 and 2 Beaches with the regiment's 3rd Battalion at the former (including 'The Point') and the 2nd Battalion at the latter. The 5th Marines 1st and 3rd Battalions landed on Orange 1 and 2 Beaches respectively. The 3rd Battalion, 7th Marines landed on Orange 3 with some of this unit's elements coming ashore amid confusion at Orange 2. The 1st Battalion, 7th Marines came ashore at Orange 3 with this regiment's 2nd Battalion held in regimental reserve until landing the next morning.

The main objective, Peleliu's airfield, was captured by the 2nd Battalion, 5th Marines later on D-Day. It was there that a Japanese tank-infantry attack was repulsed. Thereafter, the Marines' progress from D-Day to D+5 is depicted in hashed lines with the respective units' advances. Starting on D+2, the Marines began their hellacious assault on Umurbrogol Mountain at the southern end of Peleliu's expansive ridges extending up the island's north-west peninsula (see Chapter 5 for details).

0900 and 0935 hours, respectively. The 2nd Battalion, 5th Marines was the regimental reserve and came ashore soon after the initial two 5th Marines' battalions. The 5th Marines met scattered resistance and although assault craft had been hit, it was much less deadly than in the 1st Marines sector. The 3rd Battalion's commander, Lieutenant Colonel Austin C. Shofner, had his Executive Officer (XO) Major Robert M. Ash killed soon after landing. Additionally, an LVT carrying the battalion's communications equipment and signallers was destroyed on the reef, posing early unit control problems.

The 2nd Battalion, 5th Marines advanced inland into coconut groves, which provided vegetative cover, and without any gaps in the Marine line, this unit reached its initial objective, the south-western end of the airfield.

Hanneken's 7th Marines landed with two battalions in column on Orange Beach 3, the extreme right flank of the 1st Marine Division's amphibious assault, with his 3rd Battalion landing there at 0830 hours amid confusion as some elements came ashore at Orange Beach 2 in the 5th Marines sector because of heavy anti-boat shelling by the Japanese causing the amphibious tractor drivers to veer to the left. At 1030 hours, the 1st Battalion, 7th Marines landed on Orange Beach 3 with the 2nd Battalion held in reserve for landing on the morning of D+1. The 3rd Battalion received heavy artillery and mortar fire enfilading their landing beach from Ngarmoked Island at Peleliu's southern tip.

A Japanese AT ditch, located a short distance inland from Orange Beach 3, intended as an obstacle, afforded the 3rd Battalion some cover during its advance off the beach as well as a battalion CP. As the 3rd Battalion moved inland, it joined up with the advancing 3rd Battalion, 5th Marines. By mid-morning of D-Day, the companies of the 3rd Battalion were encountering Japanese resistance from gun fortifications and blockhouses near the ruined enemy barracks and had to await tank support to reduce the enemy positions.

The 1st Battalion, 7th Marines landed at 1030 hours and initially met light resistance, which intensified as they moved south. Then they reached an inland swamp that was not on the Marines' maps. The right or southern half of the battalion, in its attempt to negotiate the swamp, found that the only trail around it was heavily defended by the enemy, causing a delay of several hours in reaching their objective.

The D-Day gains by the 1st Marine Division were fewer than planned. Some units made inland progress and reached objectives; however, major issues included manoeuvring amid unfamiliar terrain which was not present on maps and, more perilously, concealed Japanese infantry. Also, gaps between the Marine units developed because of combat, scrub jungle, a swamp and disrupted communications.

Brigadier General Smith was ashore throughout the night of D-Day as the 1st Marine Division held a beachhead of 3,000 yards in length and on average 500 yards in depth. They were in control of the southern half of the airfield and had a lodgement on Peleliu's east coast. The 11th Marines had some of its 75mm pack howitzers and 105mm howitzers in position and sighted. The cost for the first day and night's lodgement, which fell below the predicted gains, was 210 Marines killed in action or missing (presumed dead) and 900 wounded. Not accounted for in these figures was the combat fatigue, the effects of excess heat (over 100° F at midday) and extreme humidity, along with lack of water.

The Marines noted that concentrated naval and aerial bombardment failed to eliminate many enemy strongpoints of resistance on D-Day. With so many Marine tracked vehicles lost to enemy anti-boat artillery shelling, reinforcements from the transports evacuation of wounded as well as moving ammunition, supplies and water to the front-line Marines were hampered. Water delivery to the Marine riflemen would continue to be a nagging problem until engineers discovered that they could drill wells to obviate the water supply issue.

Japanese D-Day Counterattack

On D-Day, Lieutenant Colonel Robert W. Boyd's 1st Battalion, 5th Marines along with Lieutenant Colonel Honsowetz's 2nd Battalion, 1st Marines were at the centre of a Japanese tank-infantry counterattack that began to develop at 1600 hours. Neither unit had advanced since late morning and both battalions were dug in parallel to the secondary cross-runway of the airfield.

At 1630 hours, the Japanese opened up with heavy mortar and artillery fire on the Orange Beaches and a few minutes later, a Japanese infantry company began to form up just north of the airfield. A well-planned, well-organized attack without surprise by thirteen Japanese tanks of the 14th Division Tank Company and a company of infantry from the 1st Battalion of the IJA 2nd IR was a complete failure. The Japanese Type 95 (1935) *Ha-Go* light tanks, which were under-armoured, were easily penetrated by Marine 37mm AT guns. Also, Marine bazooka teams and M4 medium tanks of Companies A and B, 1st Marine TB destroyed most of the Japanese armour, while the Marine riflemen killed the Japanese infantry and any enemy tank crewmen that survived.

The Japanese infantry did not attack in a tightly-bunched manner, but maintained dispersion and used ground-cover shell-holes for limited protection. Many Japanese infantrymen rode atop the backs of the *Ha-Go* tanks, which raced ahead of the remaining enemy infantry so one could not support the other's advance. Some of the Japanese light tanks that were not immediately destroyed struck the 1st Battalion, 5th Marines line in a sector held by a platoon of Company B and overran them. Although two of the tanks did reach the beach, they too were destroyed after causing only minor damage.

Another major Japanese infantry attack supported by two tanks was launched at 1750 hours at the juncture of the 1st and 5th Marines. The 1st Marines received the major thrust of the attack. The M4 75mm guns destroyed the two Japanese tanks, while Marine automatic weapons annihilated the infantry before they reached the Marine lines. A final daytime attack by Japanese infantry and two more tanks was launched at the junction of the 1st and 2nd Battalions, 5th Marines but it ended as the others. Sporadic Japanese infiltration continued throughout the night with a number of Marines killed. At dawn, the 1st Battalion, 5th Marines was hit again by two tanks supported by infantry, but was easily repulsed. Colonel Nakagawa was now devoid of any armour.

There were some attacks at 'The Point' against Captain Hunt's 1st Marines company, which left only eighteen effective riflemen by D+1. The Japanese also mounted several attacks against the 3rd Battalion, 7th Marines that were dug in at the far south of the division's line. These enemy thrusts continued for four hours from the swamp and incurred heavy Japanese casualties.

US Army's 81st Division Assault and Conquest of Angaur and Ulithi

The revised STALEMATE II called for the invasion and securing of Peleliu before Angaur was to be assaulted so that the latter island would be isolated from Japanese reinforcements from either Peleliu or Babelthuap. Angaur's pre-invasion importance was limited; however, American planners did not want it as a Japanese base to attack Peleliu after the Marine landings. Also, Nimitz wanted to construct a bomber airfield on Angaur's lowlands, but strategically it was not an important aerodrome.

Major General Paul Mueller, the 81st's CG, was tasked with Angaur's capture. In addition to Angaur amphibious invasion with the 321st and 322nd IRs, Halsey ordered Mueller to attack Ulithi Atoll with his 323rd IR. Preliminary bombardment of Angaur began on 12 September with USN gunfire from a battleship, four cruisers and five destroyers. These vessels supported Angaur's invasion until it was captured eight days later. For the Ulithi assault, 200 miles to the north and scheduled for 21 September, the USN utilized one cruiser, nine destroyers, two high-speed troop transports, 5 attack transports and 12 landing craft.

On 16 September, Rupertus gave his erroneous assurance that Peleliu would be secured in a few days. Thus IIIAC commander, Major General Geiger, released the Army's 81st Division as his 'floating reserve' to commence the Angaur and Ulithi Atoll attacks. The next day, on 17 September at 0730 hours, supporting naval gunfire and fighter-bomber sorties raked Angaur's landing beaches. LVTs of the 321st IR's two assault battalions, supported by rocket-firing LCIs, landed on Blue Beach. Moments later the 322nd IR assaulted Red Beach. Both 81st Division landing beaches lacked extensive surrounding coral reef, thereby enabling flat-bottom assault craft to come ashore. The 323rd IR, in transports that would soon depart for Ulithi Atoll, was stationed off Angaur's west coast as a feint.

The Angaur landings were met with only sporadic automatic weapons fire from the Japanese, as Major Ushio Goto sequestered his reinforced battalion (approximately 1,400 troops) from the IJA 14th Division's 59th IR for tenacious dug-in combat in the north-west corner of the island. Also, Goto incorrectly anticipated that the two US Army IRs would assault excellent beaches on the island's south-east coast, Green Beaches 1 and 2. It was there that Goto sowed minefields and constructed some formidable steel-reinforced concrete fortifications containing anti-boat ordnance and MGs. Both the 321st and 322nd IRs moved quickly off the beach inland through denser vegetation as LCVPs, LCMs and LSTs reached the shore soon after the infantry to offload bulldozers to cut roads through the jungle growth inland.

On D+1, both 81st IRs advanced with tank support to the north and west of Angaur, where the Japanese formed their final redoubt. By the afternoon of 18 September, the 322nd IR reached the phosphate plant to the north to Saipan Town's north-east. On 19 September, after Japanese nocturnal infiltrations and limited counterattacks, the 321st IR drove southward and bisected Angaur after eliminating Japanese defensive positions. On 20 September, the last pockets of enemy resistance in the south were overcome by the 321st IR, while the 322nd commenced the reduction of the final redoubt, the Romauldo Pocket, which was formed by a series of rugged coral ridges.

Due to combat inexperience, limited Japanese counterattacks/infiltration, heat, humidity and dense vegetation, Angaur was not declared secure until the morning of 20 September. Major Goto was killed in a cave complex on 19 September and three days later, organized resistance on Angaur ended. This was fortuitous since on 19 September, Geiger contacted Mueller that he needed to have the 81st Division's 321st IR re-deployed to Peleliu to assist the 1st Marine Division there. It would not be until one month later, on 21 October, that the last remnant of Japanese resistance was overcome by the 322nd IR.

The Army's 81st Division's 321st and 322nd IRs lost 260 men killed and in excess of 1,300 wounded in combat. The Japanese suffered more than 1,300 men killed and a few score taken prisoner.

With the situation on Peleliu and Angaur reportedly stable, Geiger's final IIIAC reserve, the 81st's 323rd IR, was dispatched to Ulithi Atoll on 19 September. The landing was unopposed on 22 September as Ulithi Atoll's airfield and seaplane base were seized. Nimitz obtained his fleet anchorage for future operations while a Marine air base and naval seaplane base were established.

(**Opposite, above**) Two USN cruisers are shown in pre-invasion bombardment position off Peleliu on 15 September 1944. Naval estimates of enemy target destruction were exaggerated since the Japanese local commanders built many bombproof redoubts and excavated numerous inland caves to shield waiting infantry and ordnance. *(NARA)*

(**Opposite, below**) Two USN LCI-Rockets (R) are shown firing their projectiles at Peleliu's enemy positions during the naval pre-invasion bombardment. The LCI(R) had a crew of three officers and thirty-one enlisted seamen, six 5in rocket-launchers and assorted AA guns. The LCI(R) had to manoeuvre to aim the rockets as the launchers were fixed to the deck. During launching, the crew was below decks to avoid the rocket engines' blast. *(NARA)*

(**Above**) A USN SBD Dauntless dive-bombing squadron is shown above a carrier to start Peleliu's pre-invasion aerial attack on 15 September. These USN scout/dive-bombers were work-horses during the Pacific War with their bomb load along with two forward-firing 0.50in-calibre M2 Browning MGs and rear mobile 0.30in-calibre MGs. *(NARA)*

(**Above**) Two LVT(A) 4 assault craft of the 3rd Armoured Amphibious Tractor Battalion (Prov) are shown during their run-in onto Peleliu's beaches at H-Hour on 15 September. The LVT(A) 4 had an M8 HMC turret with a 75mm howitzer to provide fire support for the assaulting Marine rifle companies against entrenched Japanese fortifications until Marine M4 medium tanks arrived. *(NARA)*

(**Opposite, above**) Black smoke is seen rising along Peleliu's assault beaches at H-Hour on 15 September with scores of tracked amphibious vehicles carrying the Marines to shore. Two USN destroyers (background) provided 5in supporting naval gunfire. *(NARA)*

(**Opposite, below**) Marines in their LCVPs are shown during the run-in to the transfer line where they boarded amphibious tractors (LVTs) of the 1st, 6th and 8th Amphibious Tractor Battalions to make the final assault onto the Peleliu beaches on 15 September. The flat-bottomed 'Higgins Boats' had difficulty crossing the coral reef necessitating the transfer. *(NARA)*

KA20-10

(**Opposite, above**) Elements of the 1st and 3rd Battalions, 7th Marines are shown taking cover from Japanese MG, mortar and anti-boat artillery fire at Orange Beach 3, the division's extreme right on D-Day. Smoke is seen billowing from disabled LVTs and LVT(A) 4s (background) hit by Japanese anti-boat artillery from enemy strongpoints to the south near Ngarmoked Island. *(NARA)*

(**Opposite, below**) In this iconic Joe Rosenthal combat photograph, Marines are shown disembarking from their amphibious tractors at H-Hour on 15 September. Several tractors have been disabled, both on and offshore, by enemy artillery. *(NARA)*

(**Above**) Marines are shown taking cover behind a disabled DUKW on an assault beach. Three disabled amphibious tractors are seen burning in the background, while on the far right an LVT(A) 4 (background, right) attempted to get ashore. Offshore, other assault vessels and destroyers provided supporting gunfire on targets identified by shore observers. *(NARA)*

(**Opposite, above**) A camouflaged Japanese 47mm Type 1 AT gun is shown here. Artillery like this created havoc among the landing craft, disabling over a score of them on D-Day. This formidable AT weapon, with a high muzzle velocity, entered service in 1941, replacing the more common Type 94 37mm version. The 47mm AP shell was able to penetrate an American M4 medium tank at 800 yards. *(NARA)*

(**Opposite, below**) An amphibious tractor destroyed by Japanese land mines is shown on an assault beach. Lieutenant Colonel Nakagawa, commander of the 14th Division's 2nd IR (Reinforced), had his men sow all potential landing sites with mines, which inflicted considerable damage on assault tractors and armour. *(NARA)*

(**Above**) Marines are seen here using a disabled LVT(A) 1, named 'The Bloody Trail', for cover to return fire on Japanese fortified positions on 15 September. The LVT(A) 1 was armed with a 37mm main turret gun and 0.30 and 0.5in-calibre MGs. In the foreground is a 55-gallon fuel drum that was for 'Water Only'. As delivery of these water cans was delayed because of destroyed and disabled amphibious tractors, thirst was a major problem for the Marines pushing inland. *(NARA)*

(**Opposite, above**) A disabled armoured tracked amphibious vehicle is shown serving as a point of protection from enemy gun and sniper fire for Navy Corpsmen and Marine SBs to assemble wounded for evacuation on D-Day. These armoured amphibians also provided much-needed firepower with either their 37mm or 75mm howitzer turret guns. *(NARA)*

(**Above**) A Marine is seen here using the crest of a sand and coral hillock for cover in order to fire his Thompson 0.45in-calibre SMG at the Japanese defenders. All positions of cover on the beaches, such as hillocks, tank traps and shell-holes, were more desirable than the open beach under enemy mortar and MG fire. *(NARA)*

(**Opposite, below**) African-American Marines from Field Depot and Service Battalion companies provided a much-needed role as SBs. Also, as sufficient numbers of riflemen waned due to casualties, these Marines grabbed rifles (above) to serve as infantry reinforcements. Major General Rupertus praised these African-American Marines and presented them with a valorous citation after the battle. *(NARA)*

(**Opposite, above**) Two Marines have come under withering enemy fire just inland from the assault beach with shattered palm trees and some dense brush giving them some concealment on D-Day. The Marine on the right was attempting to deepen his cover by moving sand and coral away with his left hand as he held his M1 0.30in-calibre carbine in his right. *(NARA)*

(**Opposite, below**) Elements of the 3rd Battalion, 1st Marines are shown taking cover on White Beach 1 (foreground). Other Marines are seen moving against hellacious fire from Japanese positions within and atop a 30ft previously unidentified ridge ('The Point') at the northernmost part of the division's left flank on D-Day. Several hours and scores of 1st Marine casualties were needed to finally secure the enemy position from the rear. *(NARA)*

(**Above**) Marines just inland from the beach have dropped for ground cover against Japanese snipers. A Marine M4 medium tank, which arrived in one of the later assault waves, is seen moving forward to eliminate the enemy positions. *(NARA)*

A Marine 37mm AT gun is shown in brush at the airfields' edge near a destroyed Japanese bomber. Bombarded Japanese administration buildings are seen in the background. An advantage of the Marine 37mm AT gun was its portability without need for vehicle support. When not firing AP shells but rather canister, this AT gun functioned as a 'giant shotgun' against massed enemy infantry attacks. *(NARA)*

Wounded Marines are shown getting medical attention at the recently-captured airfield in the shade of a destroyed Japanese bomber. The D-Day Japanese counterattack by a rifle company of the 1st Battalion, 2nd IR along with the IJA 14th Division Tank Company from north of the airfield produced significant casualties among the 1st Battalion, 5th Marines; however, it was contained by the Marines' heavy weapons and the timely arrival of eight M4 medium tanks of Companies A and B of the 1st Marine TB. *(NARA)*

Two of the approximately fifteen IJA Type 95 *Ha-Go* light tanks of the 14th Division's Tank Company that were destroyed by 5th Marines' heavy weapons and M4 tanks are shown near the airfield. The charred bodies of Japanese tankers and infantrymen lay beside their destroyed armoured vehicles. *(NARA)*

Two 81st Division soldiers are seen here crouching in the LCVP for their run-in to one of the two beaches on Angaur (Red Beach and Blue Beach). The 322nd and 321st IRs made the assault on this southernmost island in the Palau Group on 17 September, while the 323rd was held in 'floating reserve' before heading for its Ulithi Atoll assault. *(NARA)*

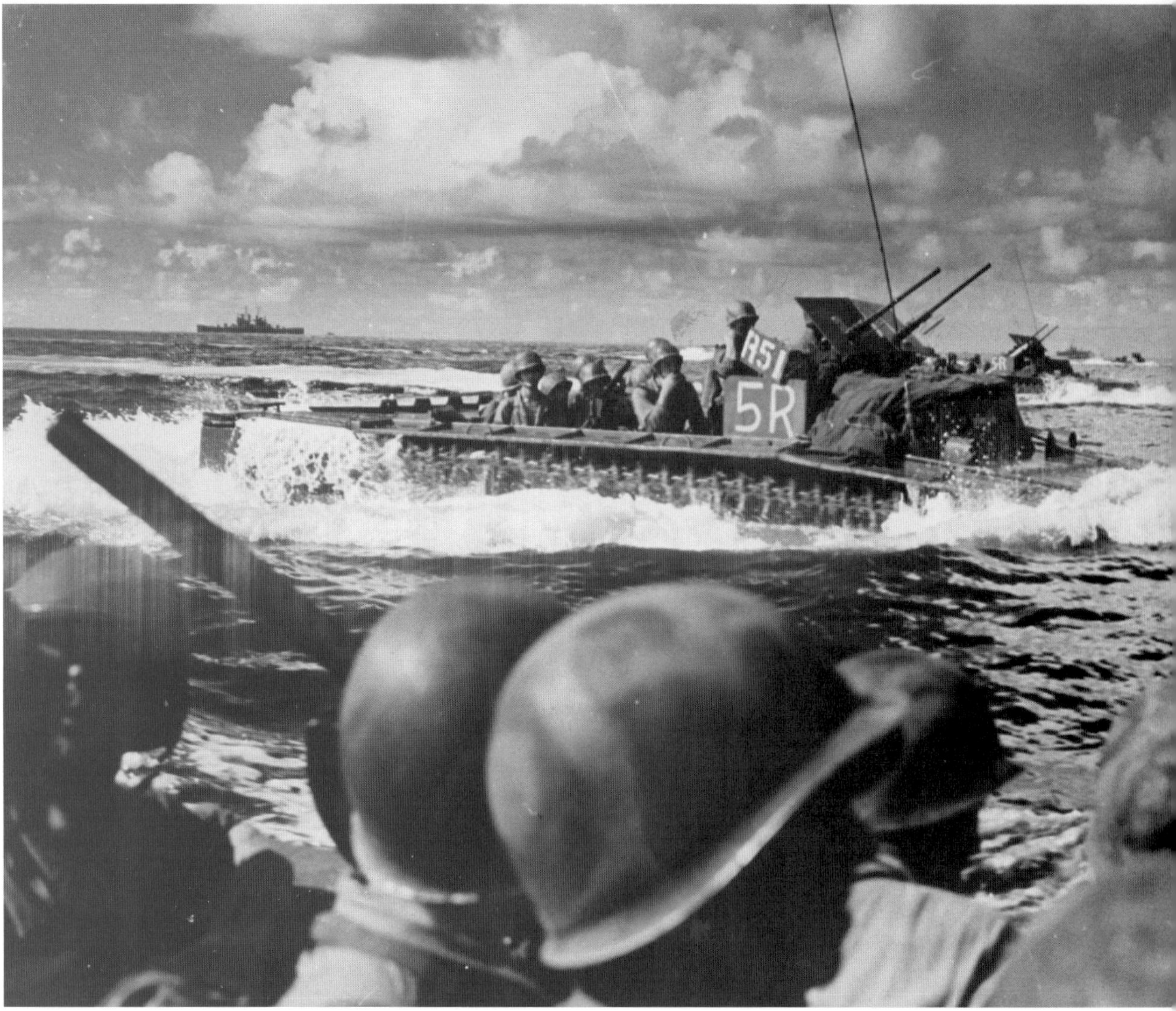

(**Above**) Soldiers from one of the two 81st Division's IRs are shown during the run-in within LVTs from companies of the Army's 726th and 776th Amphibious Tractor Battalions. The soldiers' helmet camouflage pattern can be seen in the foreground. *(NARA)*

(**Opposite, above**) A 37mm AT gun attached to a jeep is pushed ashore through the surf by 81st Division soldiers on 17 September at an Angaur landing beach. The gun disembarked over the bow ramp of the LCVP (foreground). M4 medium tanks from Companies A and B of the Army's attached 710th TB are seen already ashore. *(NARA)*

(**Opposite, below**) Soldiers from the 81st Division's 321st or 322nd IRs are shown walking upright at Angaur's shoreline from their LCVPs on D-Day, 17 September. Their assault was virtually unopposed as the Japanese battalion-strength garrison was to defend a redoubt in the north-west sector of the island. Major Goto Ushio commanded the 1,400 troops of his 1st Battalion, IJA 59th IR (Reinforced) detached from the IJA 14th Division. *(NARA)*

(**Above**) LSTs with their bow ramps open are shown disembarking vehicles at the shoreline, while pontoon bridges extended more offshore to other transports to hasten unloading soon after H-Hour on D-Day. *(NARA)*

(**Opposite, above**) Soldiers of the 81st Division's 323rd IR are shown during their run-in within LVTs to a landing beach in Ulithi Atoll, 370 miles to the north-east of Peleliu. The American infantrymen and some field artillerymen landed on 22 September against no opposition. *(NARA)*

(**Opposite, below**) Two 323rd IR soldiers are shown staring through a ruined reinforced concrete wall on Ulithi on 22 September. The soldiers found Ulithi's airfield and seaplane base abandoned by the Japanese. One soldier (foreground) is seen holding an M1 0.30in-calibre carbine, while the other (right) has an M3 0.45in-calibre SMG, also called a 'Grease Gun' because of its cylindrical appearance, tapered barrel and long box magazine at the front and bottom of the weapon. This SMG, which entered US Army service in December 1942, was cheaper to produce and lighter than the Thompson M1928A1 SMG of the same calibre, the latter being the US military's standard SMG at the start of the war. *(NARA)*

Chapter Five

Hellacious Combat on Peleliu

Major Frank O. Hough (USMCR) compartmentalized the Peleliu campaign into four operational phases. The first comprised the D-Day (15 September 1944) landings. The second operational phase spanned from D+1 to D+7 and consisted of eliminating Japanese resistance by the 7th Marines along Peleliu's south coupled with the northward advance of the 5th and 1st Marines against a well-armed entrenched enemy at the start of Umurbrogol Mountain. The 81st Division's 321st IR began relieving the 1st Marines on Peleliu on 22 September. The third operational phase, from D+8 to D+15, involved the continued reduction of enemy defences along the Umurbrogol Mountain's numerous ridges and a further drive north to capture the airfield and eliminate Japanese resistance on Ngesebus Island. The fourth operational interval encompassed D+14 to D+30, which involved the continued operations of the 5th and 7th Marines among Umurbrogol Mountain's heavily-defended ridges and valleys, culminating in the relief and departure of the remainder of the 1st Marine Division on 15 October. The final operations on Peleliu until the island was deemed secure on 27 November were conducted by the other IRs of the 81st Division.

Second Operational Phase, D+1 to D+7

The Marines, after taking heavy casualties on the D-Day assault beaches, isolated the IJA battalion defending the southern zone of the island. This development, along with the failed limited IJA D-Day counterattack, compelled Colonel Nakagawa to make suicidal defensive stands in the formidable ridge terrain of Peleliu to exact a high casualty count among the Americans.

7th Marines Advance to the South

Beginning at 0800 hours on D+1, following an enormous naval gun bombardment, the Marine assault commenced on all fronts. The 7th Marines were to reduce Japanese positions in the south, which included reinforced concrete blockhouses. The combat in the south was characterized by the 1st and 3rd Battalions of the 7th Marines advancing across low and flat terrain that contained scrub jungle overgrowth, which concealed the myriad of camouflaged, interlocking-fire Japanese fortifications that had been blasted out of the limestone bedrock and manned by the elite 3rd Battalion of the IJA 15th IR. An objective of the 3rd Battalion, 7th Marines advance on D+1 was the approaches of the landward side of the south-east promontory before digging in for the night due to excessive heat, an absence of water and gruelling combat.

The 1st Battalion, 7th Marines in a wider field of advance moved with the support of naval, artillery and air bombardment of Japanese positions on the extreme southern end of the island. On the morning of D+1, they were held up by the standard Japanese pillboxes and casemates as well as four 5in DP guns. During the night of D+1, the Japanese attempted, to no avail, to regain Ngarmoked Island from the south-west promontory to enfilade the Marine assault beaches from the flank and rear.

The 2nd Battalion, 7th Marines, acting as divisional reserve, came ashore at Orange Beach 3 during the morning of D+1. Instead of moving south with the 7th Marines' two other battalions, the 2nd Battalion deployed to White Beach 2 to assist the hard-pressed 1st Marines for the duration of this second operational phase.

On D+2, the 3rd Battalion, 7th Marines began advancing with their infantry weapons and armoured vehicle gun suppressive fire across the spit onto the south-east promontory after clearing a Japanese minefield. Within three hours, most of the enemy positions were eliminated and Marine gunners were now able to fire their ordnance across the lagoon onto the south-west promontory.

Also on D+2, the 1st Battalion attacked the south-west promontory on Ngarmoked Island, which was the larger of the two promontories with more rugged and higher terrain as well as being laced with many stronger fortifications. Fighting the Japanese defenders continued throughout the entire day, despite use of 37mm guns, M4 tanks and LVT(A)s. A renewed 1st Battalion, 7th Marines' attack commenced during the morning of D+3 and continued, despite more than 350 Japanese being killed. At 1500 hours, following the suicide of a score of Japanese officers, the 7th Marines completed their mission to clear the south of Peleliu.

5th Marines Advance to the North

Despite a Japanese artillery shell that directly hit the 5th Marines' CP, injuring Colonel Harris's knee, on D+1, and having been subjected to intense dawn enemy gunfire from ridges and woods to the north and east onto the flat and open airfield terrain that they captured on D-Day, this Marine regiment was ready for its advance. The 5th Marines moved north-east into the largest divisional zone of action.

The 1st Battalion advanced past the entire northern portion of the airfield, reaching the hangar area and dug in at an AT ditch for the night. The 2nd Battalion made slower progress with woods, jungle and the edge of a mangrove swamp to the airfield's east. This area concealed many Japanese infantrymen that were defeated, often in close combat, amid terrain where tanks could not penetrate. The 3rd Battalion saw limited action on D+1 with the other two battalions' advance and that of the 7th Marines moving first eastward and then to the south.

By D+2, the 5th Marines moved on to face the ridge system, the stoutest Japanese defences, which began at the barracks just north-west of the airfield and continued along Peleliu's north-western peninsula. The 3rd Battalion, 5th Marines, which relieved the 1st Battalion, encountered increasingly heavy enemy shelling from these heights, often in the absence of any cover. The 2nd Battalion, 5th Marines, on the right, had the advantage of concealment from enemy artillery fire within the woods, although the terrain was more difficult to advance through with limited enemy resistance on the ground.

By D+3, progress of the 5th Marines slowed as the regiment had as a left boundary the East Road, which meandered along the eastern base of Umurbrogol Mountain. Fire from these numerous ridges further to the west and north hampered elements of the 2nd and 3rd Battalions, 5th Marines that were moving out in the open. Other companies of the 2nd Battalion reached a road leading eastward to Ngardololok, which was inland to heavily-fortified but abandoned Purple Beach on Peleliu's east coast and closely bordered by swamps. Seizure of this area was an important objective of the two advancing battalions of the 5th Marines.

On D+3, with the southern end of Peleliu secure, the 3rd Battalion, 7th Marines took over the swamp area from the 1st Battalion, 5th Marines, enabling the latter battalion to re-join its regiment for the upcoming further advance.

On D+4 and D+5, units of the 2nd Battalion, 5th Marines, after having secured the northern tip of the north-eastern peninsula, moved on to seize the unoccupied Island A and then Ngabad Island. This action concluded the 5th Marine's mission during this second operational phase on Peleliu.

1st Marines Actions in the West

Company K, 1st Marines bore the brunt of the Peleliu's D-Day ferocity. After having captured 'The Point' on the far left of the division's beachhead and defended it against a Japanese counterattack of 350 infantrymen during the late evening hours of D+1, Company K, which started the invasion with 235 men, now had only 78 survivors of the combat.

On D+1, the 2nd Battalion, 1st Marines made excellent progress from the bloody beachhead crossing the western end of the airfield. However, the 3rd Battalion on the left made little progress. The 1st Battalion, which was regimental reserve, attacked from the beachhead in the early afternoon, and with some armoured support, Companies B and C captured a major portion of a ridge to their front. Other 1st Marines units encountered the reinforced concrete buildings at one corner of the airfield. Close combat with the remaining Japanese infantry at these buildings ensued.

The enemy resistance was most tenacious at the junction of the East and West Roads at the base of Umurbrogol Mountain behind the airfield administration buildings in the 2nd Battalion, 1st Marines sector. Umurbrogol Mountain was a name appearing on early maps, but applied generally to the north-western peninsula's entire ridge and hill system. Hills 200 and 210 were two forward points extending south from the main mass of 'Five Sisters'; the latter originally called 'Bloody Nose Ridge' by the initial Marine assailants.

Up until D+2, the 1st Marines incurred more than 1,000 casualties. This regiment now began to have its 2nd Battalion encounter the start of Umurbrogol Mountain beyond the airfield and administration buildings. To aid the 1st Marines, the 2nd Battalion, 7th Marines, which was re-deployed on D+1, joined the fray. The Assistant Division Commander, Brigadier General Oliver P. Smith, knew that there were dozens of caves and crevices serving as natural pillboxes among the ridges and ravines there. The Japanese had mutually-supporting positions in the limestone and coral structures that housed riflemen, machine-gunners, mortars, rockets and field-pieces. From some of the caves, the Japanese gunners ran their weapons out to the aperture of the structure, fired their round and then retreated back into the rocky shelter before the Marines could react.

After capturing the main road junction, the 2nd Battalion, 1st Marines was now astride the East Road, a main track, which ran from the administrative area through the village of Asias and along the narrow flat terrain between the swamps and the eastern base of Umurbrogol Mountain. The village of Asias, just to the airfield's north, was located in the flat terrain below Hill 200. The East Road angled across Peleliu's north-west peninsula to join the West Road near the Radio Station to the north.

Lieutenant Colonel Russell E. Honsowetz's 2nd Battalion, 1st Marines assaulted Hill 200 at the base of Umurbrogol Mountain that paralleled the East Road against intense fire from MGs, mountain guns and DP pieces from more than thirty Japanese-manned caves. Honsowetz's Marines incurred many casualties scaling this height along with several disabled M4 tanks and LVT(A)s, aptly dubbing it 'Suicide Ridge'. Nonetheless, Hill 200 was taken by nightfall. Now the Marines contended with nearby Hill 210 that paralleled Hill 200 to the west with numerous Japanese infantrymen in the ravine separating the two heights. In addition, the Japanese were firing artillery, MGs and mortars from nearby Hill 210. Honsowetz's Marines were forced to withdraw under this withering enemy fire. Repeated attacks were to be made on Hill 200 ('Suicide Ridge') and nearby heights over the next three days.

With the heavy casualty toll, the 1st Marines' unit commanders put every available man in the line for the D+3 assault, which began at 0700 hours following a thirty-minute preparatory bombardment by naval and artillery fire and aerial sorties. The 2nd Battalions of the 1st and 7th Marines finally captured Hill 210. Elements of the

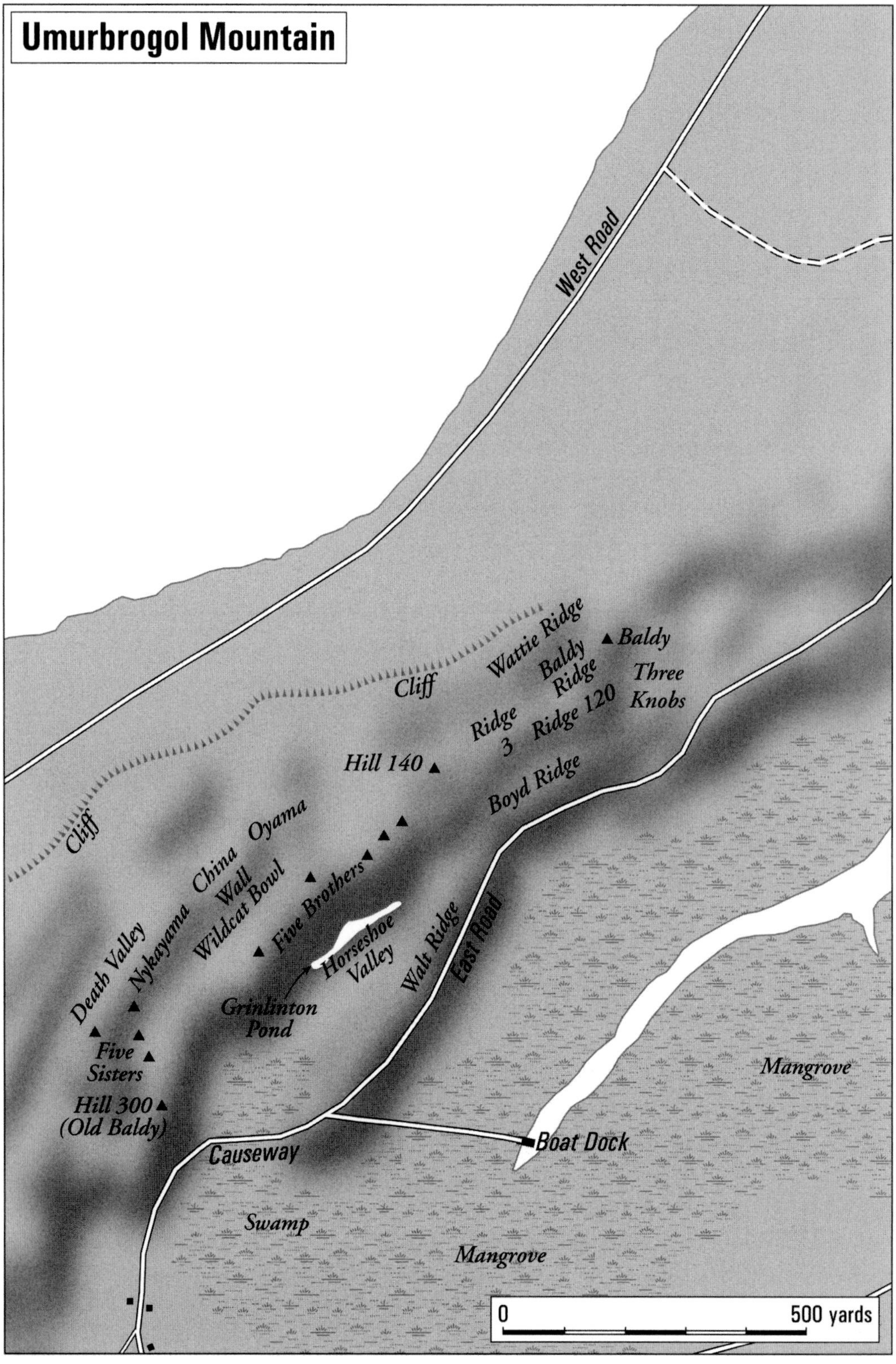
Umurbrogol Mountain
West Road
Cliff
Cliff
Wattie Ridge
Baldy
Baldy Ridge
Three Knobs
Ridge 3
Ridge 120
Hill 140
Boyd Ridge
Oyama
China Wall
Wildcat Bowl
Five Brothers
Nykayama
Death Valley
Horseshoe Valley
Walt Ridge
East Road
Grinlinton Pond
Five Sisters
Hill 300 (Old Baldy)
Causeway
Boat Dock
Mangrove
Swamp
Mangrove
0
500 yards

2nd Battalion, 1st Marines were able to capture Hill 205 slightly forward and to the right of Hill 210 with light casualties.

On D+4, the 1st Marines advanced at 0700 hours after artillery, mortars and naval gunfire opened up between 0620 and 0645 hours. The 2nd Battalion, 7th Marines made extremely slow progress in their north-eastward attack as Japanese resistance in the heights above stiffened considerably. On the right, the 2nd Battalion, 1st Marines also made limited advances until by noon it was repulsed at the 'Five Sisters', which comprised part of the southern end of Umurbrogol Mountain, by fanatical Japanese resistance. This ridge formation, with its sheer southern face, in contrast to the other ridges' topography, ran transverse of the island, in effect forming a wall barring passage northward. If one summit was reached, the next could not be directly attacked due to the precipitous ravines between them. The 'Five Sisters' were not finally secured until later in the campaign.

Also, on D+4, Captain Everett P. Pope, leading Company C, 2nd Battalion, 1st Marines was ordered to seize Hill 100 (also referred to as Walt Ridge), which dominated the East Road and the swampy terrain to the battalion's right front. Hill 100 was not a hill, but rather the forward nose of Walt Ridge. Initially, repulsed by Japanese machine-gunners in pillboxes, Pope moved across a road with M4 tank support. This road, called 'the Causeway' or 'Horseshoe Causeway', angled sharply to the east across the mouth of a draw called 'Horseshoe Valley', a rough arc from the East Road across the southern end of the swamp which fringed the inlet running northward. Hill 100 (Walt Ridge) dominated 'the Causeway'. The first M4 medium tank to attempt the Causeway slipped over one side and became immobilized. A second M4 slipped off on the other side, thus blocking the narrow approach. Nonetheless, Company C made repeated squad-level rushes to the foot of Walt Ridge, which they assaulted with only mortars and MGs. The Japanese shelled them

---

Map 8. Umurbrogol Mountain. The 'Horseshoe Valley' was the most expedient way to enter the Umurbrogol Pocket from the south-east. There, a secondary road became a dead end in the valley. The eastern wall of the Umurbrogol Pocket was Walt Ridge with its Hill 100 southern nose. Running parallel to the west of Walt Ridge was another formation, 'Five Brothers'. Hill 140, Ridge 3 and Boyd Ridge, the latter a part of the eastern wall, were separated from Walt Ridge by a steep ravine.

To the 'Horseshoe Valley's' west and separated from it by the 'Five Brothers' was another topographic feature called 'Wildcat Bowl' named after the 81st (Wildcat) Division. The western boundary of the 'Wildcat Bowl' was the 'China Wall' (also named by the 81st Division), which was a double-crested ridge that extended northward from the 'Five Sisters', the latter just to the north-east of the towering Hill 300 ('Old Baldy'). A narrow ravine known as 'Death Valley' skirted the western base of the 'China Wall'. 'Death Valley' separated 'China Wall' from the high coral formations that dominated the West Road. To the north of 'Horseshoe Valley' were ridges that were more proximate to each other and named Wattie Ridge, 'Baldy', 'Baldy Ridge', Ridge 120 and 'Three Knobs'. Some of the heaviest but successful Marine action occurred here. The Japanese defenders in the Umurbrogol Pocket were essentially stationary, but very adept at killing and wounding American forces and stalling Peleliu's conquest. *(Meridian Mapping)*

from adjacent ridges and made counterattacks throughout the night of D+4. At dawn on D+5, Pope, with only fifteen men left, withdrew to the main line across the swamp. Pope received the Medal of Honor for his gallantry during the abortive seizure of Walt Ridge.

On 20 September (D+5), the recapture of Walt Ridge was the 1st Marines' main objective with all resources committed to the attack, including all HQ personnel. Heavy Marine casualties and losses in armoured vehicles occurred as the low terrain of attack again drew Japanese cross-fire from the ridges above. With a total 1st Marines' campaign casualty count of 1,749 riflemen and officers, the regiment was temporarily a spent force, despite having killed 3,942 Japanese and captured 50 reinforced fortifications and more than 140 defended caves.

With southern Peleliu now taken over by 11th Marines' artillery positions, the 1st and 3rd Battalions, 7th Marines relieved the 1st and 2nd Battalions, 1st Marines along with the 2nd Battalion, 7th Marines during the late afternoon of 20 September (D+5). Renewed attacks along the East Road by the fresher 7th Marines' two battalions stalled under intense Japanese mortar and MG fire from heights above that was zoned in on the eastern face of Walt Ridge.

For the remainder of this operational phase, the 7th Marines and the remaining 3rd Battalion, 1st Marines attacked these Japanese-defended ridges. On D+7, elements of the 7th Marines first entered 'Death Valley', to the north of 'Five Sisters', which referred to the low ground walled in by coral ridges with dug-in enemy positions firing into it from all angles. The 7th Marines' units were attempting to seize 'Five Sisters' from the south-west. According to the Japanese, American attempts to capture Hill 300 ('Five Sisters') and Hill 100 (Walt Ridge) were unsuccessful, although Japanese casualties were extremely heavy. The 1st Marine Division's northward drive was halted by the enemy. However, during this second operational phase, all of southern Peleliu was captured, the high ground immediately dominating the airfield was in Marine possession, and the airfield was available for base development.

Third Operational Phase, D+8 to D+15

The third operational phase was from D+8 to D+15, which involved the isolation of enemy ridge defences along Umurbrogol Mountain and the further drive north to capture the airfield and eliminate Japanese resistance on Ngesebus Island.

The isolation of the Umurbrogol Mountain ridges was to be given to the 81st Division's 321st IR with the assistance of the 7th Marines. On 23 September (D+8), the 2nd Battalion, 321st IR moved up the west shore and relieved the 1st Marines. The 3rd Battalion, 321st IR followed and was prepared for action, while this Army regiment's 1st Battalion was held in reserve.

On D+9, the 2nd Battalion, 321st IR moved forward after naval gunfire and aerial bombardment. Moving along the shore to the west of a low coral ridge, elements of this battalion made good progress through to the West Road coastal village of Garekoru after capturing some Japanese defensive positions. This advance outpaced the movements of the 3rd Battalion, 7th Marines and the initial one by the 3rd Battalion, 321st IR, creating a confused and indecisive day for these latter two battalions. By the evening of 24 September, other companies of the 321st IR were gaining ground to the top of Hill 100 (Walt Ridge) and resisted local Japanese counterattacks. The enemy strength in this section of Umurbrogol Mountain, the 'Umurbrogol Pocket', was estimated at 3,000 troops. The drive of the units from the 321st IR and elements of the 7th Marines from the south-east was to isolate the separate ridges in the Umurbrogol Pocket.

Elsewhere, on the afternoon of 25 September, the 5th Marines, which were widely deployed across the region of eastern Peleliu, now passed through the Garekoru lines of the 321st IR, situated along the West Road, and attacked towards the tip of the north-western peninsula.

The high ground of Peleliu's north-western peninsula is divided into three areas. Southernmost and most formidable was Umurbrogol Mountain. The term 'mountain' is actually a misnomer since it is not one height but a series of closely-packed hills and ridges, replete with caves. Kamilianlul Mountain, also a misnomer, is a continuation of Umurbrogol Mountain with lower, narrower and less rugged heights. The broad saddle of Kamilianlul Mountain separated it from Amiangal Mountain, the north-west peninsula's northernmost formation.

On 26 September, elements of the 321st IR captured Hill B situated near the East Road and Walt Ridge, thereby isolating the Umurbrogol Pocket with its mutually-supporting Japanese defensive positions from the south-east. The 321st IR destruction of the suicidal Japanese defenders on Hill B gave American forces control of all of Peleliu northward up to the region where the 5th Marines were attacking the phosphate refinery. All that was left to the Japanese defence on Peleliu's main sector was the Umurbrogol Pocket.

On 27 September, elements of the 5th Marines spent most of the day advancing along the West Road towards the phosphate refinery opposite Ngesebus Island. There, the road was blocked by a large AT ditch which prevented Marine tanks from moving up to give the riflemen the necessary support and protection, so the sole functioning M4 tank/bulldozer of the 1st Tank Battalion moved forward under enemy fire to fill the gap so that the armour could move forward.

Other units of the 2nd Battalion, 5th Marines during the mid-afternoon of 27 September attacked the large cave blocking the lowlands sector of northern Peleliu. The Japanese caves here were constructed by IJN units before Colonel Nakagawa's arrival. Each cave had many entrances along with different levels, which created a maze to withstand direct gunfire. Cave openings and tiers had to be destroyed by Marine demolition teams. The Marines were receiving artillery fire from

Japanese batteries on Ngesebus Island that had survived American artillery and air sorties. Nonetheless, by 29 September, the 2nd Battalion, 5th Marines had secured Peleliu's extreme northern tip.

Also on 29 September, the 2nd Battalion, 5th Marines, supported by tanks, attacked southward towards Hill Row, east of Amiangal Mountain and bordering on swampy terrain. This locale was now filled with Japanese infantry that had been driven out of their more formidable defences.

On 30 September, patrols from the 1st Battalion, 5th Marines, pushing north from the Radio Station on the eastern side of the north-western peninsula, met up with Company G of the 2nd Battalion, 5th Marines moving southward through the swampy jungle terrain east of Amiangal Mountain. Northern Peleliu was now in Marine hands and the 5th Marines gave their positions to 321st IR units.

Eliminating the 'Umurbrogol Pocket' (see Map 8 for ridge locales)

From 27 September through to 15 October, both Marine and Army units, then solely 81st Infantry Division formations (15 October to 27 November) launched repeated attacks to eliminate the waning but suicidal Japanese defenders holed up in their positions within the maze of caves, ridges with sheer cliffs and ravines of the Umurbrogol Pocket. The natural caves were not as large or elaborate as those constructed by the IJN in the northernmost ridges of the island. The highest elevation reached no more than 300ft but the faces of the ridges were sheer. Again, the defences were constructed to bring mutually-supporting fire on the flanks or rear of approaching American units. Ultimately, it was the infantry and 11th Marines using hoisted 37mm AT guns and 75mm pack howitzers to fire point-blank, especially with WP rounds, into the mouths of Japanese caves that reduced these defensive positions. M4 medium tanks and LVT-mounted flame-throwers were also vital in destroying tenaciously-defended caves and crevices. Air sorties with 500lb and 1,000lb bombs as well as napalm slackened Japanese resistance in the Umurbrogol Pocket. Naval gunfire and plunging ground artillery fire were ineffective, except for keeping the Japanese holed up during the bombardment.

On 29 September, the 7th Marines attacked the Umurbrogol Pocket after relieving the 321st IR facing the northern perimeter of the 'Pocket'. Elements of the 3rd Battalion, 7th Marines had already isolated the 'Pocket' to the south and east. The 7th Marines' Regimental Weapons Company was assigned to contain the 'Pocket' to the south, an area of Japanese nocturnal infiltration to attack the airfield, facing the mouth of 'Horseshoe Valley' across the swamp with its left extending in front of the bases of Hill 300 ('Old Baldy') and the 'Five Sisters'. Units from the 2nd Battalion, 7th Marines were atop Hill 200 to the left of the Regimental Weapons Company and extended west to face the 'Five Sisters' and 'China Wall' across the southern entrance to 'Death Valley'. The 1st Battalion, 7th Marines drove southward along the East

Road and the ridges immediately adjacent to it with the 3rd Battalion, 7th Marines to their right.

Amid these hills, ravines and valleys, the Japanese exercised extreme fire discipline as to not give their positions away to the advancing Marines. Since Colonel Nakagawa lacked troop strength for mass movements within the 'Pocket', his forces continued nocturnal infiltration and very limited counterattacks.

Due to heavy losses in riflemen, the 7th Marines made little progress in advancing from 30 September to 1 October. On 3 October, a revised plan called for the 1st Battalion, 7th Marines to seize the remainder of enemy-occupied East Road areas, while the 2nd Battalion, 7th Marines would attack from the south with Walt Ridge as its objective. The 3rd Battalion was to capture Boyd Ridge from the north. The 3rd Battalion, 5th Marines was to attack the 'Five Sisters' and extend eastward in coordination with the 7th Marines' advance.

Company G from the 2nd Battalion, 7th Marines easily reached the crest of Walt Ridge during the morning of 3 October; however, they then came under intense fire from Japanese positions atop 'Five Brothers' across 'Horseshoe Valley'. The Marines dug in, awaiting tanks and engineers. Later in the day, companies from the 3rd Battalion, 7th Marines made it to the summit of Boyd Ridge. Although the 3rd Battalion, 5th Marines seized four of the 'Five Sisters', withering enemy fire caused this battalion to withdraw and set up a defensive line for the night approximately 100 yards from their previous start line. However, many Japanese positions were eliminated in the 5th Marines' attack.

On 4 October, which was to be the last attack for the 7th Marines, the 3rd Battalion moved on gaps between the now-captured Walt and Boyd Ridges, as well as among the other prominences further along the East Road to the north-east. Through these gaps, Japanese artillery fire still dominated areas of the East Road. The Marines suffered grievously from well-disciplined Japanese automatic weapons, 20mm cannons and mortars in the vicinity of Ridge 120, 'Baldy' and 'Three Knobs'. The losses among the 7th Marines companies were staggering. The 7th Marines, no longer able to function as an assault unit due to casualties, was relieved by the 5th Marines on 5 October.

An offensive by the 3rd Battalion, 5th Marines accompanied by Army tanks that began on 7 October moved into the mouth of 'Horseshoe Valley' and the 'Wildcat Bowl'. The tank-Marine infantry units attacked numerous Japanese caves within 'Horseshoe Valley', killing many Japanese defenders. The assault at 'Wildcat Bowl' was stymied. Combat among the other hills to Boyd Ridge's north-east that previously decimated units of the 7th Marines were assaulted by the 2nd Battalion, 5th Marines on 8–9 October, along with artillery fire and Marine Corsair sorties against the entire 'Pocket'. On 9 October, Company G's Second Lieutenant Robert Wattie led his platoon of men in the capture of the crest of a narrow ridge which formed the

(**Above**) Riflemen of the 5th Marines are seen here engaging Japanese infantrymen firing from administration and barracks buildings to the north of the airfield on D+2 near the village of Asias. The 5th Marines' next objective on D+2 was to approach the southern end of the heavily-defended Umurbrogol Mountain ridge system, which began at the barracks just north-west of the airfield and continued along Peleliu's north-western peninsula. *(NARA)*

(**Opposite, above**) A Marine 37mm AT gun is shown engaging a concrete Japanese pillbox north-east of the airfield with Hill 200 or 'Suicide Ridge' in the background. This height was attacked by the 2nd Battalion, 1st Marines from 17 to 20 September. 'Five Sisters' (originally called 'Bloody Nose Ridge'), is situated in the far right background, partially obscured by the tree. *(NARA)*

(**Opposite, below**) An aerial view shows the southern end of Umurbrogol Mountain as it extends towards the ridges of the Umurbrogol Pocket. 'Five Sisters' and Hill 300 ('Old Baldy') are indicated (left). In the centre foreground dominating southern Peleliu's road junction are Hills 200 ('Suicide Ridge') and 210 with a ravine separating the two heights. The East Road (far right) parallels Hill 100 (Walt Ridge). To the left of Hill 100 (Walt Ridge) is 'Horseshoe Valley' (indicated), with the freshwater Grinlinton Pond in its centre. To the left of the pond is 'Five Brothers', while at the northern end of the valley is Hill 140. A large swamp is present in the right foreground, which channelled the Marines' attacks towards the ridgeline to get to the West Road (upper right) and other north-west peninsula objectives along with Ngesebus and Kongauru Islands beyond. *(NARA)*

Five Sisters
Hill 300 or Old Baldy
WILDCAT BOWL

A Marine column is shown marching single-file along a road towards the junction of two tracks. The track to the right wound around the swamp to become the East Road, while the left track skirted Hills 200 ('Suicide Ridge') and 210 towards 'Horseshoe Valley' between Walt Ridge and 'Five Brothers'. *(NARA)*

Two determined 1st Marines riflemen are immortalized by a photographer during the combat for 'Five Sisters' (or 'Bloody Nose Ridge'), which was initially assaulted on D+4. 'Five Sisters' southern face was sheer and ran transverse of the other ridges, thereby forming a wall barring passage northward. As one summit was reached, the next could not be directly attacked due to the precipitous ravines between them. The 'Five Sisters' would not be secured until later in the campaign. *(NARA)*

A unit of the 2nd Battalion, 1st Marines is seen observing the preparatory artillery and mortar barrage before assaulting Hill 200 ('Suicide Ridge') on D+2. Lieutenant Colonel Russell E. Honsowetz, who was to win a Navy Cross for gallantry for this four-day action, led his men through a minefield before reaching the crest of the ridge by nightfall. The Japanese commenced pre-registered artillery shelling, which inflicted many casualties among the Marines and as casualties mounted, Honsowetz withdrew his force. *(NARA)*

(**Above**) Riflemen from the 2nd Battalion, 1st Marines are shown using an assortment of weapons against dug-in Japanese defenders on Hill 200 ('Suicide Ridge'). The Marine (far right) is shown holding his M1 Garand rifle with an attachment at the barrel's crown to fire grenades. A Marine (centre) is seen tossing a 'Molotov cocktail' incendiary. A lit burner to light the incendiary's wick before tossing it is shown (centre foreground). According to Lieutenant Colonel Russell E. Honsowetz, CO 2nd Battalion, 1st Marines noted that the Japanese were invisible except for small counterattacks. Cliffs and swamps precluded flank attacks to assault Japanese mortars, which were hammering the Marines. Honsowetz's Marines continued advancing, despite mounting casualties. *(NARA)*

(**Opposite, above**) A Marine is shown here throwing a hand grenade at an enemy position during the four-day combat action at Hill 200 ('Suicide Ridge'). The Japanese had mortars and 37mm mountain guns within their caves, the latter having knocked out a tank and two armoured amphibious tracked vehicles. Naval gunfire and 11th Marines' 75mm and 105mm howitzers often proved ineffective at reducing the positions. It was left to Marines with their array of incendiary devices, grenades and explosives to do so. *(NARA)*

(**Opposite, below**) A Marine is shown firing his M1 0.30in-calibre carbine rifle at a Japanese cave's entrance after detonation of a TNT satchel. Marine demolition teams moved yard by yard through enemy fire to set their TNT charges and then quickly scamper for cover from snipers as well as the explosion, if the Japanese did not disconnect the fuse before the charge went off. One morning a squad of Marines set out before dawn to blast caves. An hour later five of the Marines were dead or wounded. Another six-man demolition team was credited with blasting more than eighty Japanese caves and pillboxes on Hill 200 ('Suicide Ridge'). *(NARA)*

(**Above**) A Marine BAR gunner is shown firing on Japanese positions from behind a tree trunk on a ridge face on Umurbrogol Mountain with many crevices and cave openings visible. A second Marine is firing his M1 Garand rifle (left background), while the corpse of a Japanese soldier is seen lying to the left of the BAR-wielding Marine. Despite tanks, LVT flame-throwers, air sorties and naval fire missions, it was the Marine or Army infantryman with their personal combat weapon that ultimately wrested the Japanese defenders from their coral and limestone fortifications. *(NARA)*

(**Opposite, above**) Soldiers of the 81st Division are situated atop one of Peleliu's innumerable ridges during the advance up the island's north-west peninsula. From these scaled heights, small pieces of ordnance and mortars were able to rain fire on Japanese troop concentrations below or across the ravines to nearby enemy-held ridges. *(NARA)*

(**Opposite, below**) A Marine bazooka team is shown firing their projectile charge at a Japanese sniper position from the top of one ridge towards another. This weapon provided the American forces with a direct-fire rocket, which at short range was more accurate on target and immediate than plunging mortar or artillery rounds. This model M1A1, which appeared from 1944 onward with the purpose of being an AT weapon, fired a shaped charge with HE and WP warheads, which were both suitable against Japanese defences. *(NARA)*

An 11th Marines' battery of 75mm pack howitzers is shown on a fire mission against Japanese positions. In addition to being in the open on flat terrain or within sandbag revetments, the pack howitzer could be manhandled up the ridges of Umurbrogol Mountain to bombard enemy defences across ravines on nearby heights. *(NARA)*

A Marine with a non-lethal head wound is shown being escorted down the rough, uneven terrain of a ridge that was just scaled. If American bombardment did not create a 'moonscape' to the faces of enemy-held ridges, Japanese troops before the invasion removed vegetation in front of caves and crevices to provide clear fields of fire on advancing American units. *(NARA)*

(**Above**) African-American SBs are shown carrying the body of one of their fallen Marines back to the rear for identification and burial. It was Marine custom to retrieve the bodies of their fallen comrades; however, in certain situations during the combat on the ridges of Umurbrogol Mountain, tactical withdrawal necessitated leaving the corpses on the battlefield for later retrieval. *(NARA)*

(**Opposite, above**) An 81st Division soldier is seen searching for lurking Japanese in the wrecked Post Office building of Saipan Town, Angaur's capital, on 18 September (D+1). Saipan Town was situated midway along the island's western coast. The 322nd IR pushed west from Red Beach on D+1 and reached the phosphate plant, just to the north of Saipan Town. *(NARA)*

(**Opposite, below**) Soldiers from the 322nd IR are shown here advancing alongside an M4 medium tank of the 710th TB over one of Angaur's narrow-gauge railways, which linked the eastern and northern coasts through the north-central part of the island. The Japanese had 1,400 men of the 1st Battalion, IJA 59th IR, under the command of Major Goto, to defend Angaur. *(NARA)*

A Japanese gun position caused 81st Division soldiers to pause their advance along the narrow-gauge railway. An M4 of the 710th TB was needed to reduce the position. The tanks were invaluable as they blasted suspicious-looking clumps of trees, caves and bunkers that were opposing the 322nd IR's advance. *(NARA)*

Soldiers from the 81st Division are shown watching the detonation of one of their explosive satchels in one of the caves on north-western Angaur. Other infantrymen are atop the rocky outcrop to fire on any escaping Japanese. The northern part of Angaur consists of extremely rugged coral and limestone ridges up to 200ft in height. The remainder of the island was undulating, relatively flat terrain. *(NARA)*

Soldiers of the 321st IR are shown marching onto Peleliu on 22 September via a pontoon causeway built across the reef to facilitate their landing. The Army infantrymen began arriving on this date to assist the Marines, who had incurred horrific casualties during the invasion's first week, especially among Colonel Puller's 1st Marines. *(NARA)*

A Marine and two 81st Division soldiers are shown waiting for Japanese survivors to come out after an explosive satchel was detonated at the mouth of a cave. The American forces were in the painful process of reducing the Umurbrogol Pocket one cave and one ridge at a time during the third operational phase for Peleliu. *(NARA)*

282146

(**Opposite, above**) A squad of 81st Division soldiers is shown firing their M1 0.3in-calibre carbines at Japanese positions dug-in above on a ridgeline. The M1 carbine was lighter and made up, in part, for its lower stopping-power than a M1 Garand rifle with a fifteen-round detachable external magazine (centre soldier). *(NARA)*

(**Above**) Two 81st Division soldiers are seen taking cover beside their M3 White half-track as they were alert for enemy snipers amid the phosphate plant ruins at the tip of Peleliu's north-west peninsula during the campaign's third operational phase. A third soldier is shown manning a 0.50in-calibre HMG on a monopod mount at the rear of the half-track. *(NARA)*

(**Opposite, below**) Several Marines are shown taking cover behind rocks at the mouth of an enemy cave in the Umurbrogol Pocket. The oil drums containing gasoline were about to be detonated to burn out the cave. IJN personnel constructed cave defences with tiers to minimize the effect of direct gunfire, so incendiary devices were employed by American troops to penetrate deeper into excavated defences. *(NARA)*

A Marine detachment is shown here advancing up the face of one of their last ascents up an occupied ridge on Peleliu before their relief by the 81st Division. The campaign to reduce the Japanese defences on the ridges of the Umurbrogol Pocket and elsewhere was costly for both the 1st Marine Division and soldiers of the 81st Infantry Division. *(NARA)*

Epilogue

Peleliu's intense combat, involving the US 1st Marine and Army's 81st Divisions pitted against a Japanese foe that preferred complete annihilation as an alternative to surrender, did not finally end until 27 November 1944. More than 25,000 other Japanese troops had been bypassed and isolated on the much larger northern Palau island of Babelthuap and other smaller, nearby islands in the Palau groups.

The campaign was drawn out, despite successful but costly seizure of the Marine assault beaches, principally due to Peleliu's terrain and Japanese defensive works that minimized their losses to overwhelming USN gunfire, the latter proving to be initially ineffective at reducing enemy fortifications. These Japanese defensive fortifications, drilled and excavated before the invasion, were successful at enfilading both Marine flanks at the assault beaches, inflicting heavy casualties among the Marine riflemen as well as assault vehicles and boats. Although the assault beaches were secured, Marine operations on D-Day were hampered by surviving encased Japanese artillery. Later on, Marine-directed targets were better neutralized by accurate and effective naval fire missions and aerial sorties.

Apart from an IJA infantry company-sized tank counterattack, mounted with less than a score of light tanks, during the late afternoon of D-Day, there were no futile Japanese *banzai* charges. Lieutenant Colonel Nakagawa's strategy ensured that both American Marines and soldiers paid a maximal toll of KIA and wounded against Peleliu's suicidal Japanese defenders holed up in their ridgeline caves, crevices and fortifications.

The 1st Marine Division losses were 1,252 killed and 5,274 wounded or missing. The Army's 81st Division lost 542 soldiers killed and 2,736 wounded. The total of almost 10,000 American casualties, although numerically less than the 14,000 Japanese troops killed, foreshadowed how the suicidal Japanese defensive paradigm was to delay the American advance on the island groups yet to be assaulted.

The benefits of the Palau Islands victory have remained dubious. Mindanao and other southern Philippine Islands were bypassed by MacArthur in favour of a direct amphibious assault on Leyte. However, with this move by the SWPA force, the use of the Palaus as a base for Japanese heavy bombers against a MacArthur-led Philippine Islands invasion was negated. In addition, for more than two months before Peleliu was finally secured by 81st Division soldiers on 27 November, the enemy garrison of 25,000 troops in the other Palau Islands to the north was isolated for the remainder of the Pacific War. Although these IJA and IJN forces, under General Inoue, were only 500 miles from the upcoming nexus of combat, the Philippines, for practical purposes they may as well have been in the more remote areas of Imperial Japan's conquests during the high-water mark of 1941–42 conquests that were now also bypassed to 'wither on the vine'.

Marine Sergeant Robert Martin of New York is shown blowing colours on his bugle at a 1st Marine Division flag-raising ceremony at the divisional CP near Peleliu's airfield on 27 September. Four days earlier, the 81st Division's 321st IR began to relieve the battered 1st Marines, which sustained heavy casualties during the assault on D-Day on the 1st Marine Division's left and in combat for the hills and ridges comprising Umurbrogol Mountain's southern end of the extensive ridgeline that ran up the north-west peninsula of the island. *(NARA)*

Colonel Lewis 'Chesty' Puller (left), CO 1st Marines, with Major General William Rupertus, CG 1st Marine Division at burial ceremonies to honour the fallen Marines on Peleliu. More than 1,250 Marines were either KIA, died of wounds or were missing in action. Of the 1st Marine Division's three regiments, Puller's 1st Marines incurred the most fatalities. The 81st Infantry Division suffered 208 soldiers KIA on Peleliu and another 196 who died in combat on Angaur. *(NARA)*

In another iconic Joe Rosenthal photograph, Navy Corpsmen are shown assisting wounded and dead Marines on a Peleliu assault beach near an LVT 2 soon after the assault forces moved inland. The 1st Marine Division suffered approximately 5,300 wounded during the entire campaign. The 81st Infantry Division had more than 2,600 soldiers wounded on both Peleliu and Angaur. *(NARA)*

While the fighting continued on Peleliu to reduce the Umurbrogol Pocket, US Sixth Army troops led by General Walter Krueger, under MacArthur's overall SWPA command, landed on Leyte Island in the Philippine Archipelago on 20 October 1944. The seizure of Peleliu was conducted to secure MacArthur's 'right flank' for the initial planned Philippine assault on Mindanao to the south; however, that island was bypassed. *(NARA)*

General Douglas A. MacArthur, CG of SWPA, is seen here walking through the surf from an LCVP onto Leyte to announce his return to the Philippines. On the far left is the Philippines president, Sergio Osmeña, along with Lieutenant General Richard Sunderland (right of MacArthur), the long-serving COS from the Pacific War's beginning. Since Mindanao was initially bypassed with the Leyte assault, controversy lingers as to the strategic importance of the Peleliu and Angaur seizures with their tremendous casualty figures. What might have happened with the Leyte assault if Peleliu and Angaur were not invaded just over a month before MacArthur's return remains uncertain. *(NARA)*

Bibliography

Diamond, Jon, *New Guinea: The Allied Jungle Campaign in World War II* (Stackpole Books, Guilford, 2015).

Diamond, Jon, *Guadalcanal: The American Campaign against Japan in WWII* (Stackpole Books, Guilford, 2017).

Diamond, Jon, *The War in the South Pacific* (Pen & Sword Books, Barnsley, 2017).

Diamond, Jon, *The Battle of Okinawa: The Pacific War's Last Invasion* (Pen & Sword Books, Barnsley, 2019).

Diamond, Jon, *MacArthur's Papua New Guinea Offensive 1942–1943* (Pen & Sword Books, Barnsley, 2020).

Falk, Stanley, *Bloodiest Victory. Palaus: America's Pacific Offensive 1944* (*Ballantine's Illustrated History of the Violent Century*, Random House, New York, 1974).

Gailey, Harry A., *Peleliu 1944* (Nautical & Aviation Publishing Company of America, Annapolis, 1983).

Garand, G.W. and Strobridge, T.R., *History of the US Marine Corps Operations in World War II*, Vol. IV, *Western Pacific Operations* (Historical Branch, G-3 Division, Headquarters, USMC, Washington, D.C., 1971).

Hough, Frank O., *The Assault on Peleliu* (Historical Division, USMC, Washington, D.C., 1950).

Leckie, Robert, *Strong Men Armed* (Random House, New York, 1962).

Leckie, Robert, *Delivered From Evil* (Harper & Row Publishers, Inc., New York, 1987).

Moran, Jim and Rottman, Gordon L., *Peleliu 1944* (Osprey Publishing, Oxford, 2002).

Sledge, E.B., *With the Old Breed: At Peleliu and Okinawa* (Presidio Press, New York, 1981).

Sloan, Bill, *Brotherhood of Heroes: The Marines at Peleliu, 1944 – The Bloodiest Battle of the Pacific War* (Simon & Schuster, 2005).

Smith, Robert Ross, *The War in the Pacific: The Approach to the Philippines* (Center of Military History, United States Army, Washington, D.C., 1984).

Wheeler, Richard, *A Special Valor: The U.S. Marines & the Pacific War* (Castle Books, Edison, 1996).

Notes

Notes

Notes

Notes

Notes